The Story of Ireland's Only
Steeplejill

*Breeda en memory
of Move to Ennis!
May you always be Lucky.*

The Story of Ireland's Only
Steeplejill

Angela Collins O'Mahony

Angela Collins O'Mahony

MERCIER PRESS
IRISH PUBLISHER – IRISH STORY

Front cover image: climbing Cork County Hall, 1985
Back cover images (clockwise from top left): Killaloe Lakeside Hotel, 2 August 1966; climbing using the old bosum chair system; installing a radome on top of a tower; inspecting a steel chimney; Susan, me and Taoiseach Enda Kenny

MERCIER PRESS
Cork
www.mercierpress.ie

ISBN: 978 1 78117 446 3

10 9 8 7 6 5 4 3 2 1

A CIP record for this title is available from the British Library.

Printed and bound in the EU.

I dedicate this book to John, my husband of fifty years;
to our children, Susan, John, Martina and Hilda;
and to our grandchildren, Karen, Andy, Emma and Kate

Contents

Prologue 9

1   Growing Up in Kilkishen 11

2   Working Life and Romance 35

3   Starting Collins Steeplejacks 61

4   Essco and Radomes 87

5   The Telephone Call from Mr Cohen 115

6   Clonlara and Beyond 137

7   Cork Great Race 163

8   Beating Colon Cancer 189

9   Looking Back and Lessons Learned 213

Acknowledgements 221

Prologue

I recall being conferred with an honorary doctorate in Dublin Castle like it was yesterday. The then Taoiseach, Albert Reynolds, presented the parchment to me. I was with my family and friends among some of the greatest minds of Ireland. I found it hard to contain my inner joy, but, despite the great ceremony, flashing cameras and smiling faces, my thoughts travelled back to my humble beginnings and to my first childhood memory.

1

Growing Up in Kilkishen

When I was three years old or so, my mother sat me on a chair and dressed me in new socks, new shoes and a new dress and cardigan. I can still remember the feel of the socks as she rolled them onto my feet. When she had finished, she admired her work, stood me at the front door and told me she was going to cycle to visit her family and was taking me with her. She warned me not to move or dirty my dress.

For a while I did as I was told, but soon got bored and ran off to shush away the hens and chickens that were pecking around on the ground. I did a twirl in the middle of them and fell flat on my face in the mucky yard. I was covered in mud and really upset, and my mother came running to me. She tried to brush me down, and I knew by her face that she was very disappointed. It was the end of our outing, because there was no other dress. That is my earliest memory.

My father was Martin Collins, born in 1901 at Enagh, Kilkishen, Co. Clare. He was over thirty years old when he met my mother, Mary Kate McNamara. Dances were held at crossroads back then, and the Gullet, in Cratloe, Co. Clare, was where my parents first met. We knew, from the conversations we heard over the years, that they married for love. The wedding was held in January 1933 in my mother's local church in Cratloe. The wedding photograph shows her and her bridesmaid dressed in winter coats and my dad and his best man in suits. They looked so happy. She was twenty-seven years old, and Dad was thirty-three.

My grandfather, Matthew McNamara, was from Gallows Hill, a few hundred metres from the Gullet crossroads where my parents met. He inherited the family farm from his father, and, when doing the family tree, I saw they were on that land back as far as I could trace, to the 1770s. He married Honora Sheedy from Truach, Clonlara, Co. Clare. They had five children. Patrick, the eldest, went into the priesthood but left later, married his neighbour and went to live in Dublin. Jimmy was next, and he remained on the farm. My mother, Mary Kate, came in the middle. Annie was next, and she also married her neighbour, but unfortunately she had no family. The youngest was Jack, who inherited the farm in later years. He also married his neighbour, and they had one daughter, Catherine, and though she is only a first cousin and ten years younger than me, she is like my sister.

I remember my mother being so happy on the days when Jack and Jimmy, Annie and Patrick, along with Patrick's wife and four sons, met at Gallows Hill. I was about four or five at the time, and Catherine was not yet born. I used to watch the boys playing happily until I joined them, and then they quickly scattered out of sight, hiding around the trams of hay.

My dad's father, Patrick Collins, married Bridget Collins (no relation), from Cappanalaght, Gallows Hill, Cratloe, Co.

Clare. They had seventeen children, two of whom died in infancy. Dad was the youngest. His oldest brother, Michael, emigrated to England, where he found work and married. He died, aged forty-two, leaving a young family. Another brother travelled to Australia.

Most of the family went to the United States of America. The parents saved the fare to send their oldest daughter, Katherine, there. She married an Englishman named Cutler, and they went into the harness business. The business did well, because she was able to return to visit and, later, to bring her brother out to join her. Then that brother brought the next, and that one the next, and that continued until only my father, his sister Delia and their parents remained in Ireland.

Dad often talked of his and Delia's heartbreak as they said goodbye to their siblings, never to see them again. After having had such a large family, my grandparents had no Irish grandchildren. Delia never married, and Dad was single at the time of their deaths in April and July 1926, when he inherited the family home and farm.

In those days, when marrying into land, it was the custom that the bride brought a dowry with her. Cash was scarce, so the dowry could be made up of animals or a combination of animals and cash. Its size depended on the size of the future husband's farm, which had to be assessed by the bride's father. During their frequent rows, Mam would tell us that Dad had misled her father when he came to view the farm. Apparently Dad had opened an entrance to a neighbour's field, to pretend he had more land than he actually had, and borrowed some additional animals for the day, purely with the intention of procuring a bigger dowry. It had worked, according to Mam. Her father had been tricked, and she had brought too many cows with her.

My parents had six children. Paddy was born in December 1933, Martin in December 1935 and Bridget Anne in May 1937. Fifteen months later, in July 1938, Michael arrived and Sean the following year in December. I was the youngest, born in May 1943 after a break of three years and five months.

My grandparents, Matthew and Honora, my aunt Annie and my uncles Jack and Jimmy often visited Mam at Enagh. When Paddy was a couple of years old, they used to take him to their home in Gallows Hill for short breaks. They became very fond of him, eventually keeping him permanently. This helped Mam, as she had so many children to mind and cows to milk, as well as caring for my aunt Delia, who was unable to walk, having been born with her knees bent, and had to be carried everywhere. My grandmother Honora died in Gallows Hill in 1940, before I was born, but I have memories of my grandfather, Matthew, visiting us on his ass and cart. He died in 1959.

In 1944, my sister Bridget Anne became ill and was taken to Ennis General Hospital, ten miles from our house. There was no public transport and few people had cars. Mam cycled, but was heartbroken she could not stay by Bridget Anne's bedside. Dad visited by horse and cart and by bike. He told us he had heard her crying out in pain before he reached her bedside.

After visiting, he used to call to the Franciscan monastery in Ennis to ask the monks to pray either for her recovery or that God would take her to Heaven. One day, a monk told him to visit on the following Tuesday at 2.30 p.m. and that she would die then. Dad went there at that time, and that was exactly what happened. He was with her when she died, on 7 November 1944. She was seven and a half years old.

Bridget Anne was buried in Clonlea graveyard with my father's parents and his brothers who had died in infancy. Dad talked of her often, but my mother never did. Neither recovered from the shock. I often found Mam crying, and, when I became an adult, I understood and tried to imagine what it was like for them to lose a child under such circumstances. During arguments, my father always said to us, 'Your mother is a changed woman.' She invariably replied, 'You have the drink to fall back on.' Drink dominated our lives from that time onwards.

Our home was the usual Irish farmhouse, with a thatched roof and three windows front and back. It had three small bedrooms and a large kitchen with a concrete floor. There was a settle-bed in the kitchen, which acted as a sideboard during the day. The fireplace was so large that as a child I could easily stand in it. If I looked up through the chimney I could see the sky. The space around the fire was whitewashed and there was a concrete hob at either side to sit on. A crane hung on the back wall to hold kettles and pots of water over the open fire. It swung back and forward as required. There was a steel oven for baking bread, usually left to the side. The teapot and a steel iron were always placed in front and were rarely put away.

There was a hen house attached to one gable end, then a calf house and, further down, a small storeroom and then a piggery. Across the road there was another shed, with no windows, just stone walls and a galvanised roof. It had many uses. Mam put us in there when she went shopping. She gave us milk and bread and bolted the door on the outside to ensure no harm came to us. I have no bad memories of this, and I am sure she was only away for a couple of hours.

The thatched roof of the farmhouse leaked often. Dad did repair it, but probably not often enough. In around 1947, the rotted roof collapsed – old timbers, thatch and dust fell every-where. My brother Martin and I were in bed when I heard an unusual noise. We put our hands up as if to keep the ceil-ing from crashing down on our heads. Thankfully we escaped unharmed – that end of the house remained standing – but some of the dust and rubble fell onto our bed. The incident was very exciting to me, but left us homeless. My parents had to find a house quickly, which was difficult back then.

In the meantime, we were cared for at Ennis General Hospital. I have vague memories of being alone in a ward with three of my brothers. I remember a priest and a nun coming to give them Holy Communion. When they left, we took the sheets off the beds to put over our heads and pretend we were them. I also remember jumping from bed to bed when no one was looking. I enjoyed the time there, as it was unusual to be with my brothers in a confined area, where they had no choice but to include me in their games. Eventually our parents came and took us to temporary accommodation in Kilkishen village.

My brothers attended the three-roomed school in Kil-kishen. At first I was too young to attend, so I used to go to the wall and talk to the children in the schoolyard. I loved the village as there was so much company there. However, it did not suit my parents. They felt very squeezed, having come off the land where they were accustomed to plenty of space. They had to walk or cycle over a mile to and from the farm each day, bringing me with them.

Another unpleasant aspect of village life was that Dad was close to the pubs. Mam would give him his weekly allowance for two pints, but it was never enough. He had to get alcohol by hook or by crook, and he had many ways of getting the money for it. Going to funerals was a favourite strategy of his because he knew that there would always be a barrel of porter bought for the occasion. He attended most funerals and would cycle for miles to one.

Dad was known as a matchmaker. I remember once when he arranged for his bachelor cousin from near Ennis to come to our house and introduced him to a nearby farmer's daughter. This lady, tall and thin, attractive and hard-working, was about the same age as the cousin and would have had a handsome dowry. They seemed very suitable. The day arrived and the introduction took place, but though Dad's cousin found her pleasant he did not offer her marriage. He felt it strange she wore a headscarf indoors and that she heard noises in her ear. It put him off. It was true that when she was in our house she kept her scarf on and her hand to her ear but nowadays we would know she had tinnitus. We felt very sorry that the match was not a success as that prevented her brother being able to marry. He could not bring a strange woman into his home while his sister remained unmarried. Matchmaking took place a lot back then, and my father was very involved and had some success.

At fairs and markets, Dad sometimes helped with the wheeling and dealing. He would put in an offer to buy an animal, to get the bidding going for a seller or to bring down the price for a buyer. He was charming and had the gift of the gab. He loved when our own cattle and pigs were fat enough to be sold at the fairs. Usually boys went to the fair with their fathers, but Dad brought me with him on occasion. I was useful to run ahead of the cattle and stand at the crossroads to prevent them going in the wrong direction or trespassing into fields if gates were open.

When he had sold the animals, he would try to send me home so he could go to the pub, but Mam told me to stick with him and pester him to come home before the money was spent. One time, his cousins had their nephew with them, and we children had to wait outside the pub, sitting on the footpath. (Women and children never went into pubs in those days.) Dad kept sending out lemonade and Marietta biscuits. The first lot was well received, but soon we had had enough and wanted to go home. We occasionally peeped in and would say to each other, 'Oh, they are finishing now,' but they would place their glasses back on the counter only for them to be filled again. It was useless beckoning at Dad to come out as then he just sent out more lemonade. When he finally finished, he was very drunk. It took a long time to get him home because he kept falling and trying to get up.

Sometimes he stayed away for days and came home penniless in the middle of the night singing 'Spancil Hill' or 'The Old Woman from Wexford', if he was in jovial mood, or, if he was not, shouting a litany of abuse about something Mam had said or done, or about the neighbours, calling them land-grabbers and anything else that came to mind. When confronted next morning, he would remember nothing.

Whatever time he arrived home, he always wanted food. He would fall over a couple of times before he reached the table; then he took a long time to eat. I always thought that drink must be a funny thing: it gave you the impression that your mouth had moved from where it used to be, because Dad was never able to feed himself. I had to catch his hand and guide the fork for him.

We were afraid of him when he came home drunk. I did not want my mother in the house, as he often threatened to hurt her – and did, when she would not give him money. We often sat her on the window sill so we could push her out if he came to hit her. Other times, I begged her to take the blankets from the beds and go out to the hay barn until he was asleep. He often came out and found us, and then we had to find another place to hide. It was very tiring going to school next day having had little sleep and pretending nothing had happened. It was worse for Mam as she had so much work to do.

Dad rarely got up before 6 p.m. when the fire was on and the cows milked. He took his meals in bed and would call out to us in the kitchen to bring him whatever he needed. That was the way he lived his life.

We did have occasional happy days. Dad often took his bike apart and repaired it. When we dismantled ours, if we had difficulty getting them back together again, he always came to the rescue. He made calf baskets, put shoes on the horse and repaired the woven seats of our *súgán* chairs. He did the very necessary work of sowing crops for he knew that if there was no food for the animals he would have no money for alcohol. He found the thinning and weeding very boring and never went on his knees to do it. It was mostly left to my mother, especially after my brothers went away to work.

Once the crops were growing in the ground, Dad took things easy and went back to bed again until harvest time. Then he worked very long hours and often cut a whole field of oats or barley in a day on his own. It was very hard work and required skill, as the scythe was very dangerous. He used the horse to plough up the potatoes and take them from the ground, and we used to put them in pits to preserve them over the winter. He also ploughed up the turnips, mangels and other food crops. We loved the days in the bog when he cut turf using a *sleán* and we stooked it in piles to dry. Then we all helped to bring it home and made a reek of it at the gable end of the house. He used a billhook to cut back the hedges but often left early and Mam had to finish.

When saving hay, Dad often put me behind the rake and hay turner, which drove my mother mad, but I enjoyed it – I loved being trusted. He showed me what was dangerous, and I was careful. One day, he put me on the horse after he had removed the tack but had left the winkers on. He did not hand me the reins, and, when I leant down to reach for them, he hit the horse with something that made him bolt. The horse threw me over his head and galloped off. I fell heavily on the ground. I got to my feet, shaken and very frightened, and asked Dad why he had done it. He replied that it would teach me not to trust anyone.

When it was the time of year to go to Limerick to buy bonham pigs, Dad prepared for days before, cutting barrels in half to put the piglets into, to keep them from running away. One year – I remember the day well – we saw him off on his long journey. After he had gone, Mam prepared the shed for the piglets and talked throughout the day about the profit she would make when she had fattened them. In the evening, she cooked a nice dinner for Dad, and we walked out to the gate several times, listening for the noise of the old steel wheels of the cart on the stone road. Eventually we saw the horse in the distance walking slowly towards us. When he came to a stand-still at our gate, Dad was smiling and said 'Whoa' to the horse in a jolly voice, so we knew he was not sober.

To our horror, a couple of piglets were hanging off the end of the cart, choked. The rest had escaped. There were no piglets for fattening or selling. Dad did not realise anything was wrong until he saw our faces. It was only then that he looked back, and his expression changed instantly. The terrible sight sobered him. The joy on my mother's face changed to disgust. She just lowered her head, buried her chin in her chest and walked back to the house. I followed her, feeling pity for both of them. Her hard-earned money was spent again.

Dad tried to explain that he came out of Limerick without going to any pub and that it was only when he was near home that he had decided to go for one pint. That one led to others when friends arrived. He told us he had the barrels well covered and had ropes tied onto the pigs to keep them safe. Someone must have taken off the covers and played a trick on him. (There was always someone else to blame.) He then went into the house, went to bed and stayed there for days. Mam left home and went to her family. Dad got up out of bed eventually and went and brought her back. I was about seven and was very lonely as I thought she was never coming back, and that was the worst part.

Pigs did not have much luck with us. I remember another incident, when Dad succeeded in bringing bonhams home alive and Mam fattened them and got them ready for sale. I watched them every day and named them all. One day, one was taken away from the others, and a couple of men came to help Dad kill it. They tied its two back legs together – the screeching was frightening – and hoisted it up on a hook on the side of the shed. Then one of the men took a fierce-looking knife, went over to the pig and stuck the knife into its heart.

It was customary to leave the pig to hang for hours to let all the blood run out. Women were ready with buckets and basins to collect every drop and take it to the kitchen to make sausages and puddings, which were later divided among the helpers. Later, the men took the pig down and cut it into portions. Some pieces were hung off the ceiling over the fire to be smoked, and the rest was put in a barrel with layers of salt and left there for weeks to preserve and cure. When the work was done, we all had a delicious fry of the newly stuffed sausages, pudding, liver and kidneys with tea and bread or spuds. Everybody who had helped ate with us and got some to take home. This process was repeated on the next farm in due course.

We children were not always given the cured meat to eat because my mother sold it in order to pay bills in the local shops. We were soon back to eating mashed potato and eggs with the occasional 'spotted dog' (white bread with a few currants) when Mam baked it.

My mother was a kind and soft-hearted woman, and could laugh heartily when she had a reason, which was rare. I loved her dearly, and we got on really well. She was tall and thin, and some neighbours commented that they did not know how she managed to do so much work. Some used to say she was made of steel. She was a Trojan worker, who gave everything to her family. She spent days in the meadows thinning and weeding acres of different crops, often in very cold and wet conditions. I often sat on her back while she was doing that work, pretending she was my horse. She would laugh and never once told me to go away. When her own weeding was done, if she was short of cash, she took on contracts from other farmers. I remember one day she collected £5 for thinning a neighbour's meadow. It took her a long time, and we only had cold milk and bread to eat, but she was delighted with her money.

She did the tiresome job of milking twelve cows by hand morning and evening. I hated milking cows. We all did. When it was milking time, we used to develop headaches, sore fingers and tummy pains and had to lie down. Once Mam had finished the milking, we were miraculously cured.

She often sent me to take the cows back to the field, and that meant going along the public road, but it was quite safe as there were plenty of houses on the way. She would tell me to take my time so the cows ate the grass on the side of the road where it was green and plentiful. Ours was a small farm, and Mam wanted to save what she had.

Mam also reared hens and chickens. When they were fattened, she would walk among them, catching some, snapping their necks and hanging them on nails beside the back door to let the blood drain. Then she would drop each one into hot water, pluck off its feathers and clean it. These she brought on her bicycle to the farmers' markets at Kilkishen or Tulla, along with eggs, vegetables and homemade butter.

She often went to the farmers' market in Limerick. Sometimes she began early in the week, pulling up cabbages and potatoes and telling my brothers to cut and bag timber. She loaded it all onto the horse and cart, and anything that didn't fit she hung outside the cart. Then she tacked the horse and walked the ten miles to Limerick market, often leaving home at about 4 a.m. When she had everything sold she bought groceries, clothes and animal feed. She would arrive home weary and tell us all about her day and her delight when her work was done and she could sit on the cart to rest her feet and begin the journey home. We were always delighted to see her back because she would have plenty of fresh food with her.

Markets were not held often enough in the small villages, so she also sold her produce to local shops or from door to door. There was less competition and more profit that way. She sometimes took one of us with her. I loved when it was my turn – having to calculate how much money was owed, taking it and giving change, and then getting a toffee lollipop at the end of the day.

Mam often took me out of school on Tuesdays to go to Newmarket, a few miles away, to sell her produce. One day, the headmaster told me not to take off the same day each week as

I was missing the same subjects. When I told Mam, she was embarrassed and stopped taking me with her.

Mam also made clothes and always sewed vests from flour bags and turned the collars on shirts and coats inside out so they could be worn again. She told me that her Singer sewing machine was the first thing my father bought her after they were married. I still have it. She did all the painting and wall-papering in the house. I helped and was excited with the end result – I have loved DIY ever since.

She loved the evenings by the open fire. She used to ask Dad to read *Ireland's Own*, *Our Boys* or the *Clare Champion*. She loved hearing scary tales, such as *Kitty the Hare*, while she was resting. When there were no newspapers, she would ask Dad to tell her a story, but he usually sang. The stories were fine, but I hated listening to the same old songs. One of Dad's stories was about when he was a young man and he was sent on his horse at midnight to fetch a priest for a dying neighbour. He was told to hurry as it was urgent. When he came to a certain part of the road, the horse would not go any further. Dad told us that the Devil was stopping the horse, as he was after the soul of the dying person. I remember being gripped with fear and unable to sleep that night.

In the evenings, once the five decades of the rosary and the trimmings were over, we played draughts or Ludo until an argument broke out, and then my mother would take every-thing away. My father would join in when we played cards, especially Forty-five and Twenty-one. I often asked if I had won, and he would tell me to get a pencil and paper and add up the score. Soon I began to enjoy that.

Mam and Dad sometimes took us to visit houses where there was a gramophone. When they danced, I stopped playing to look at them. They looked lovely dancing together, and happy. I wished it could always be like that. I have only a couple of memories of them that way. They might have been from weddings, as people held the receptions in their homes in those days.

My father was always asked to dance and sing, and I remember him being coaxed to keep step dancing and then to sing a song shortly afterwards, and him saying, 'Will ye give me a chance to get my breath!' He rolled up two tea towels, crossed them on the floor in the shape of an X and then danced across and around them. When the musician played faster, he danced to keep up with him. I loved to hear everyone clapping, and I was very proud of him. Dad was an entertainer and enjoyed the attention.

In about 1950, my parents bought their first radio, which was only turned on for the news and some programmes. On the nights Din Joe's *Take the Floor* came on, Dad pulled me out on the floor to teach me to dance, and I eventually got the hang of it. The radio was a novelty and kept him home from the pub on occasion.

For years my parents had been looking for a home nearer to their farm. Then, one day, luck came their way when they met a bachelor neighbour with a bicycle business who wanted to live in the village. So they just swapped. His house was out in the countryside, in Ardane near Kilmurry, in the parish of Sixmilebridge, Co. Clare. It had a large kitchen, two small bedrooms downstairs and a larger attic bedroom upstairs, which was a novelty. There was also a field where my brothers could play hurling. The move was an improvement but still not ideal as it was half a mile from the farm. We were not in a financial position to build a new house or to repair the old one.

Ardane was very different from the village. It was quiet, and I was lonely. My brothers were at school or working, and all our immediate neighbours were either unmarried or had no children. I visited them all the time, but I missed the company of the village children. Our next-door neighbour, Mrs Stephens, taught me to knit and was a real conversationalist. We became close friends and stayed in contact right up until her death. She took an interest in us all, and in later years, when I was working, she waited at her gate to check my post-office book and make sure I was saving.

When the time came for me to go to school, I could not attend as I had ringworm on my face and head. It was very unsightly, and I felt awful. Dad travelled the county making enquiries, and then one day he told my mother to get out the iron, as he had been told of a cure. She cleaned the face of the cold steel iron, and he rolled up a newspaper tightly and placed it on the surface. He lit the newspaper and left it to burn out. It left a residue, which he applied to the ringworm. And it cured it. I can still remember the happiness I felt when my hair grew back. I looked normal, and I could go to school.

I enjoyed school, especially when I was in Mr O'Connell's classes. He was the principal and a kind, wonderful teacher. One day, my skipping rope was taken from my bicycle. Mr O'Connell immediately arranged for all the pupils to leave the classroom, with their bags. He then allowed each pupil back, one at a time, so whoever had taken it could put it back without embarrassment. No one did. Mr O'Connell did not give up. He took us outside to search around until eventually it was found under a little pile of stones.

When I was eight or nine, the time came for me to receive Holy Communion. Everyone was talking about the Big Day and their new clothes. My mother made mine: a *báinín* skirt and coat. I was expecting to visit our relations in Gallows Hill and looked forward to getting some money. There must have been a bad row the night before because neither of my parents went to Mass that morning. That in itself was unusual as it was a mortal sin to miss Mass. Mam dressed me and sent me to walk the lonely road from our house in Ardane to Kilmurry church, which was a surprise, as I had never done that before. There was no other house on our roadside between our home and the church. I was afraid but excited, so I went without any fuss.

On the journey, I realised I did not have a communion bouquet, but I saw white flowers on the bushes by the road so I climbed the ditch and picked some. They had thorns and were prickly to hold, but they looked splendid to me. I put them down in front of me in the church, and nobody noticed any difference.

After the ceremony, I saw my classmates having their pictures taken. I was ashamed to be alone and remember quietly walking away behind the crowd. I passed the large chestnut tree at the corner and walked down by the forge, happy to be out of view. I had only walked about fifty yards when our next-door neighbour, Tess McNamara, came along in her ass and trap and asked me to sit in. She had a rug over her knees, and she shared it with me. She gave me a hug, admired my suit and told me I was lovely and that God was with me. I felt great when she told me that. She handed me a shilling, and I felt greater still. We continued our journey and talked continuously until we came close to home, then I hopped out and walked down the hill to my home.

My mother took off my new clothes, veil, shoes, the lot, and put everything away carefully. I remember she was very sad. She asked no questions, but I told her about Tess McNamara bringing me home and showed her the money. That is the memory I have of my First Holy Communion. It stood to me in later life.

By this time, my aunt Delia was very frail and was spending most of her time in bed. She became ill and passed away on 3 February 1951. I remember the night they waked her in the house, and the next day a horse-drawn hearse came to take her to Kilkishen church, even though we were not in the parish at the time. Delia was buried in Clonlea with my sister Bridget Anne and Dad's parents and brothers. Even though life became easier for my mother, my aunt was sadly missed.

About that time, my father received a letter from America telling him he had inherited money from a relative. That news filled the house with happiness. My parents longed to hear how much, and decided there and then, whatever the amount, it was to be my dowry. It meant I could marry a farmer when I grew up. They must have felt they would not be able to save enough to provide me with a dowry, and now that problem was solved. When the money arrived, Mam put it in the bank in Tulla with my name on it. At the age of eight or nine I had no idea what a dowry or legacy meant, but I learned over the years because they never stopped talking about it. (When I was twenty-one, it amounted to about £450 with accumulated interest.)

Around 1956, we received wonderful news once again. A house joining onto our farm came up for sale. It belonged to Mr Martin Collins (no relation), who, when he sold it to my father, also named Martin Collins, must have caused quite the headache for the Land Registry. It had taken almost nine years for us to get back to the farm, and the move proved magical. Now we were able to go inside any time and have a cup of tea. Life was back to where it was before the thatched house collapsed.

In the mid 1950s, a group water scheme came to the area. We bought a sink and got water on tap for the first time. Later, my parents saved enough money to build a bathroom, and this was magical also. We didn't think life could get any better when we received the excellent news that electricity was coming to our area, but when the black creosoted poles were in the ground and our house was wired to take the supply, my mother would allow us to have only one bulb in the kitchen, and no plugs. She did not even fit one socket to boil a kettle, which would have made life so much easier, and resisted every pressure to do so, saying she would be disgraced if she was not able to pay the bill. And so she continued with her open fire and stayed with the old ways.

When we moved back to Kilkishen, I was in my final year at Kilmurry Primary School. I wanted to go to school nearer home, but my mother told me to finish in Kilmurry. I had a different idea. I went down to the school in Kilkishen and booked myself into Sixth Class. I came home that evening and told my parents that it made sense to change as it was a shorter journey but that I needed a note from them in order to transfer. I thought they would be angry, but they accepted my decision. I also told them that when I finished I would attend the Convent of Mercy secondary school in Tulla. I wanted an education so that I could work in an office. My mother was not impressed with my notions and told me I would go to work after completing my Primary Certificate, the same as many others. However, I nagged her continuously, and she eventually allowed me to go to secondary school.

A group of us cycled to the school in Tulla, which was about four miles away. First I would meet Mary and Berry McNamara, our neighbours. Then, in the village, we met with two more McNamara sisters, Mary and Margaret, and our neighbour, Berry Deasy. Nearer to Tulla we joined up with the Murphys, Minogues, Danaghers and Greens. There was always laughter, tricks and craic with neighbours all along the way. I loved school and the nuns and worked hard to do well. I did not get into any trouble, but when the nun was writing on the blackboard I often threw a note across to my friend and just barely missed getting caught. That was the extent of our tricks.

Most teenagers tried to get into Kilkishen village to meet each other, and I was no different, but Mam wouldn't let me. We did not have boyfriends, but, at fifteen, we were at the looking stage, laughing and talking about boys, and we needed to get together to do that. One time I told Mam I was visiting

Mrs Stephens, who lived in Ardane, but that meant turning left outside our house – and the village was to my right. I decided to cycle left, away from my ultimate destination, and to keep going until I thought she would have gone in to the house. I looked back to check and when I couldn't see her decided it was safe to turn back. When I saw the door open, I feared that Mam would hear the bicycle chain making noise, so I lifted it up on my shoulder and crept past the gate. I was doing nicely until she stepped out and caught me red-handed.

I came up with another plan and asked Mam if I could join the Legion of Mary (a Catholic organisation that helped with voluntary work), and she agreed. The local curates trained us teenagers to hold meetings and to take minutes. I enjoyed their company, and the meetings were fun as well as a way to meet teenagers my own age. Otherwise, our lives were a bit mundane.

We were warned that if we did attend a dance or céilídh we would be expelled from the convent, and, if that happened, we would be disgraced. That seemed awful at the time, but, looking back, it kept us concentrated on our education. When the famous dance bands came to the marquee in the village, once a year, I was allowed to stand outside with my friends but had to come home after an hour or so. We admired the style and the couples dancing, and longed to be grown up. I marvelled at the funny styles women wore in their hair, like plaits, braids and buns. Some backcombed their hair high and wide.

When I was fifteen, I decided that I would not stay in school to sit my Leaving Certificate and told my parents about the Limerick Business School, which offered a course in shorthand, typing and bookkeeping. If I went there and passed the exams I could get an office position. They agreed, even though it was a private college and expensive.

To get to Limerick I had to cycle about four miles from my home to Sixmilebridge and then travel ten miles by bus to Limerick. Mrs McNamara, the owner of the college, was an excellent teacher. While I loved figures, I knew I would have to work hard to keep up with the class, most of whom had their Leaving Certificate.

The wealthier students hired out typewriters on which to practise, but I stayed in the college at lunchtime to use the typewriter and did my shorthand on the bus journey as well as at home. I loved the course and knew I had made the right decision. I was very determined to get my office job.

My parents began coming to Limerick to meet me. They took me for lunch to Hogan's restaurant in High Street, which was close to the market where farmers came to sell their produce. I soon found out that they were matchmaking for me. They had gone along with my decision to get educated but figured that I would end up having children and doing housework and that education was wasting time and money. I was not on their wavelength at all. I was going on sixteen, felt I knew everything and had plans of my own.

I sat the exams and got a Distinction, but unfortunately there were no jobs right after I finished, and I had to stay home. My mother kept saying, 'Now, where did the education get you? You would have been better off if you had gone to work and saved that money and added it to your dowry so you could marry into a bigger farm.' Then she went on recommending

suitable people. Both my parents offered me the farm and suggested I marry one local man in particular. They told me with
both farms I would have a fine living and my dowry would go
with me.

That might have been my only option. Then, one day, a letter arrived from the college signed by Mrs McNamara asking
Mam to send me back. She would not charge any fee as there
were interviews coming up and she was sure I would get a
position. It is hard to explain the happiness that letter brought
as I had been full of despair until then. (I still have it, almost
fifty-five years later.)

2

Working Life and Romance

I was back at the Limerick Business School only a few days, preparing for the upcoming interviews, when I answered the door to a man of about forty-five years of age, five foot six inches tall and above average weight. He wore a moustache. He was fifteen minutes early for his 12.30 appointment with Mrs McNamara. I asked him if he could come back, but he told me that he would wait.

I was about to go back upstairs when he asked me my name and what I was doing. I told him I had completed my exams and was waiting for a job offer and that I had achieved the advanced grades in typing, shorthand and bookkeeping. I talked non-stop, not realising that he was interviewing me. At 12.30, I went up to tell Mrs McNamara that the man had arrived. She went down and came back up very quickly to tell me he was interested in employing me.

His name was Mr Daniel Lynch, and he was a steeplejack. His office was in St Joseph Street, just across the road. 'She'll do fine' was what he said to Mrs McNamara. I went with him to his office, where he showed me ledgers, bank sheets and invoices. He told me I would have to type circulars, take shorthand, send quotations and reply to letters. He would be back and forth to the office but would mostly be out on sites all around Ireland. He would pay me £1 a week wages and a bonus of 1 penny on each pound lodged. I would have no holidays; however, he would pay double wages for two weeks in lieu. I had never had a holiday, so that did not matter. I was overjoyed with the offer.

The small office had a desk, a chair, a typewriter, a filing cabinet and a paraffin-oil heater in the corner. It had one window and a galvanised roof and was built in one corner of a large builder's yard. It was not what I had expected, but I was excited to be chosen for the job. At 5.30 p.m. that evening, I left with the key and went home to dangle it with delight in front of my parents. I happily recounted every detail of my day. They appeared startled and confused.

When I went to bed that night, I could not sleep. I thought about the office and came to the conclusion that it was not where I wanted to work, and, though I was eager to be employed, I felt I could do better. My idea of an office was in some grand building downtown in Limerick.

The next morning, I cycled off as normal, but I did not go to Mr Lynch's office. Instead, I went back to the college. I told Mrs McNamara I could not work in an office with a galvanised roof. I was afraid and confused at all that had to be learned. The accounts ledger would be simple enough, but when Mr Lynch had shown me all the invoices and letters from customers and told me to reply to them, I had panicked and felt that I would not be able to do all the work without guidance.

Mrs McNamara understood because she knew my age, that it was my first job and that I would need someone to train me. To my relief, she took the office key and sent me back to class. I had thought that, having completed my exams, I was an expert on office work, but after my trip to Mr Lynch's, I realised I knew very little.

Just as I sat down, Mr Lynch arrived and asked for me. I was embarrassed and found it hard to tell him that I wanted a nicer place to work. He answered me, 'That is the reason I want you. You see, things need to be improved. I'll give you a free hand, and you can build a new office.' I thought to myself that if he was depending on me to improve things then things must be bad. I asked him who was employed before me, and he replied that he had sacked her. That frightened me even more. Then he offered me 10 shillings more per week. All of a sudden the galvanised roof was lovely and the work was no problem. He seemed very genuine and I knew I could work with him, so I returned to his office with him. I could not wait to get home to tell my parents what I had done and that I had received a hefty increase.

The next day, I was nervous and did not know where to begin so I filed invoices and read letters. If I did not know what something meant, I left it to one side. Then I opened the filing cabinet and looked at the contents. The phone rang, startling me, and I grabbed it like a hot iron. I answered it upside down, wondering where the voice was coming from, but soon figured out where the mouthpiece was. I was glad Mr Lynch was away and had not seen that I had never answered a phone before.

When I finished that evening, the place was tidy but not sorted. As the days passed, I looked at the ledgers and soon learned the difference between each one, and when post arrived I told Mr Lynch what was in it, and he instructed me what to do. I had to send out receipts and reply to letters, and he did not always dictate them, so I found that very difficult for a while. People called for cheques and left invoices, and one day a man called with a statement. I took a chance and asked how he had reached the figure, as my accounts book was different. He was kind and taught me how to enter invoices and credit notes and how to compare and reconcile his account. I was missing some documents, and he went to his company for them. Once his account was correct, I knew how to do the others. That was probably my best day, and Mr Lynch never found out that I didn't have a clue about reconciling or doing accounts. I received most of my training from people calling into the office.

Mr Lynch phoned regularly and dictated quotations, and I took them in shorthand to type up later. I was terrified at all the new words and did not dare ask him to repeat them, but I opened old files and looked for similar quotes, and on occasion I asked the steeplejacks.

It was not long before I began to take my boss's work and worries home with me. On many occasions during the Christmas period I went back to the office to see what post had come in, and if cheques were not there I would not be able to sleep. When the men arrived into the yard for materials, I tried to get them loaded quickly. I knew I would be charging per hour for each man so they needed to be on site early and produce results each day. I was very thrifty and did not waste anything as that was my background. I knew I would be the one asking the customer for payment so it was important the work was done well and on time. An honest day's work for an honest day's pay was drilled into us.

In the beginning we had two or three steeplejacks who worked for a weekly wage, but that grew to sixteen over six years. Back then, when we had very wet and windy weather, steeplejacks were off and the employer received 'wet time' from the government.

It was not always easy to get payment on time, as some customers took more than their thirty days. Other times, it was not possible to get payment if the job was not completed. While Mr Lynch was a kind and generous employer, he was a tough taskmaster if things went wrong. He often got furious if a cheque was late and said, 'Don't take wages if you don't get cheques in.' He would tell me to go to the offices of the people who owed money and 'do a sit-in' until I was paid. One time, I went to an office and waited for the payment, but when 5.30 p.m. came, I was told the cheque was not ready and that they were closing the office. With all the staff standing looking at me, I had no option but to leave. Mr Lynch was very angry and told me I would soon be out of work. I was not sure if he meant it or if it was an idle threat.

I was afraid of getting sacked like the former secretary. I appreciated I was doing different and interesting work and wanted to mind my position. My wages were more than most who had done their Leaving Certificate, and I had a bonus, which was rare. As time went by, I realised Mr Lynch was just pushing me to do my job better and get money in, and that was very good training. Cash flow was always a problem, but everyone paid in the end.

When I became more familiar with Mr Lynch, I asked about the new office. He immediately hired a local man to build it. I stayed late to help him and his friend, and I planned the decoration, bought lino floor covering and made curtains. When finished, we had two nice offices, a reception area and a bathroom, and there was still loads of space in the large yard at the rear.

Whenever Mr Lynch was in Limerick catching up on paperwork, he sent me to collect his dinner and ordered the same for me. That was a treat as I had never had fancy food. He often got me to unpack his case, do his washing and pack fresh clothes to get him ready for his next journey, but I did not mind as it trained me to be flexible and an all-rounder. Sometimes, when he was up the country, he would tell me to get prices for materials and later would call back for the answer. Even though I might be waiting on others for information, he would take no excuses. His motto was to get the job done.

His business went from strength to strength. He employed more steeplejacks and began getting larger contracts. He told me to hire a girl to assist in the office. Having plenty of contracts gave us security and time to get more work, so I sent out hundreds of circulars.

Mr Lynch knew I cycled from my home in Enagh to the bus in Sixmilebridge, and I was often drenched when I arrived at work as it was difficult to cover up on a pedal bike. He took me to look at a Vélosolex, a new kind of bicycle with a motor on the front wheel, and suggested that I buy it as it only cost £70. I ordered one there and then. I paid for it on hire purchase and used it to come from home to Limerick each day. Because I did not have to pedal, except on a steep hill, I could cover myself with a plastic cape and leggings and arrived to work dry and warm.

That motorised bicycle had other benefits, especially when I was going to dances at weekends. (I was allowed to attend dances after I left the convent.) I could pull my two friends and their bikes after me by putting a rope around my waist, which they held on to. We arrived at places much faster and could travel further. We also got strange looks when flying by other cyclists. Unfortunately, the Vélosolex broke down after a couple of months, and the supplier took it back.

It was decided then that I would move to live with my aunt Annie, who rented a room in Limerick. That proved too small so we got a larger place in Lower Mallow Street, where we had a room to cook and live in as well as a nice separate bedroom. We shared a toilet on another floor with the other tenants and got water from the tap there, as was the norm. Annie was my mother's sister and worked at Saint Camillus' Hospital in Limerick. I lived with her until she moved to another position near Lahinch, Co. Clare. I missed my parents but loved Limerick, my landlady and her family, who all lived in the building. I remained there for the following six years. I went home at weekends.

When Mr Lynch saw me coming to work on Monday mornings wet and miserable again, he told me I should get a small car. He would increase my salary and would pay expenses to help me run it. I could use the car to collect cheques, deliver materials and drive to the bank instead of walking.

My brother Michael let me drive his car once, and I drove it up on the ditch and almost crashed. Soon after that, he spent a couple of hours showing me how to steer straight while he changed gears. That was the only driving experience I had ever had, and I knew I needed more.

I could not get the thought of owning a car out of my mind and imagined being able to drive to dances and go home to take my parents to Mass. I began to realise it was a possibility: I did not drink alcohol, smoked very little and saved each week. I went and priced the smallest car I could find, which was an Austin 7. It cost £425 in 1960.

Mr Lynch was going to Lourdes on an overnight vigil to pray for a special intention and asked me if I wanted to go. I decided I would, and, while there, I would pray for a car and write a petition. It was my first time going on a pilgrimage and being in an aeroplane. Participating in the candlelight procession was very moving, joining with thousands of pilgrims from so many different countries. It was frightening to see so many invalids, and that pilgrimage put things in perspective for me.

During the night, I walked in and out of the church with Mr Lynch to stay awake. On one occasion, he knelt down and examined the lightning conductor on the church with his cigarette lighter to check how the tape was attached to the stonework. He saw an L-clip on it and told me to source the clip when I got home. So as well as praying he was trying to improve his business.

I was back at work when the salesman phoned regarding purchasing the car, and I discussed it again with Mr Lynch. We agreed that I would buy the car on hire purchase. The salesman delivered it to me at the office and asked me to drive him back to the garage. I sat into the car and said to him, 'You must tell me what to do, I am not able to drive.' Well, I never saw anyone jump out of a car so fast, and he walked back.

I went home to my rented room in Mallow Street after work, leaving my brand-new car sitting in front of the office. Later, my sister-in-law, Patsy, returned with me and stayed for hours while I practised stopping and starting and how to brake. That night, I went over it in my head, and the next morning I drove to work and never looked back. I was seventeen and could not believe my luck.

Now that I had a car, my duties expanded. I was sent up the country to deliver materials and to collect cheques as well as doing the normal errands around town. When I was sent out to sites where steeplejacks were working, I would blow the hooter to get their attention.

One day, Mr Lynch gave me a task that was to change my life forever. He sent me to deliver materials to his employees working in Mullingar, Co. Westmeath. When I arrived, they were one hundred feet up, on top of a building. I beeped the horn to attract their attention, but either they did not hear me or they were accustomed to hearing horns blowing in the towns so they did not take any notice. I wandered around the base of the building to see how the men had gone up and saw ladders attached on the side. Without thinking, I climbed up until I reached the top. I told the steeplejacks I had brought their supplies and had left them on the ground below. No one made any comment, and, as far as all were concerned, I was just doing my job – it seemed the normal thing to do. It did not occur to me that I had a head for heights.

Up on the roof, the steeplejacks explained what they were doing. Later, I learned the different methods of repairing industrial chimney stacks and removing slates before fitting new ones to roofs of convents and churches. I learned how to price the painting of a building and the different textures. I was often sent to measure a chimney and quote for its repairs. Brick chimneys could be oiled and painted, and, if cracked, we fitted steel bands on them. I also saw how to demolish brick chimney stacks and soon could price that work. I learned how to remove a steel chimney, price a new one and fit it back with guy wires. Soon I could identify the different types of paints required for the different temperatures and knew which ones lasted the longest.

It was easier for me to procure materials once I knew what they were for. Knowing how things worked made life simpler and more interesting as my employer did not have to spend time explaining those things to me any more, nor did he have to put orders through, as I had learned to do that.

Mr Lynch had purchased machines to fabricate his own steel bands, angle irons and lightning conductors, and he showed me how to use them. Eventually I got the hang of it all – except for welding. Once, when he wanted a lightning conductor, he phoned and told me to make one. I had to put the telephone out the office window and go out to the adjoining machine shop. He instructed me how to put a length of copper into the cutting machine, clamp it, start the machine and cut off three-foot pieces. He waited until I had finished the task. Then he told me to move to the next machine and to put each bar in. That machine threaded the ends of the copper rods, allowing them to be screwed into a base plate. Then I had to turn on a grinding machine, and he told me to hold each bar and twist it around until it was pointed at one end. That was tricky, as the sparks were going in all directions. The phone line often dropped, and I would have to phone him back for further instructions. When I finished, he told me to wrap one, go onto the street and ask a passer-by to help me load it into my car. Then I was to drive to Limerick Station and put it on a train for him to collect.

It was very unusual for a woman to be doing this type of work, but I was happy to learn how to make things and did not mind getting my hands dirty – probably because I had been brought up with brothers and grew up following my father about. But I preferred the office work.

As time went on, my confidence grew, and I soon knew about everything happening in the business. Driving around the country, I looked for slates missing on roofs and, if I spotted a blocked or leaking gutter, I called in to the customer and suggested what to do, telling them we could send our steeplejacks along to do the work.

One day, I was driving back to the office when a tourist bus drove out from a side street, straight into me, pushing the car a distance across Henry Street before coming to a halt in front of the General Post Office. I was badly bruised on my right side and was out of work for over a week. Our GP, Dr Houlihan, came regularly to the house in Kilkishen to treat me. Mr Lynch also came out to get the important paperwork attended to: the steeplejacks' hours had to be calculated so wages could be paid. I made every effort, using my left hand, and he did the rest. I raised invoices and he posted them; otherwise, he would not have had money for the following week. I remember getting about £200 compensation for my injuries, and Mr Lynch's car, which I had been driving that day, was written off.

That was the only time I missed work, except for a half day when I was invited to the wedding of one of the foremen. During the wedding breakfast, a telegram arrived from Mr Lynch asking me to phone the office. There was no phone, so the groom drove me to Limerick. On arrival, our boss just wanted to see a file. I pulled the file and gave the details. The groom did ask if it could not have waited, and then he and I went back to enjoy the day. Those were the times: we all jumped when told, no matter the circumstances.

On 8 May 1964, I turned twenty-one and collected my dowry, even though I had not married a farmer. I had my party in Geary's Hotel in Thomas Street, with family and friends. We had an enjoyable evening – without alcohol, as that was the custom. I felt very rich so I traded in my old Austin 7 and bought a new Vauxhall Viva. I loved my new car. It was larger and more comfortable on long journeys. I could carry more materials as it had a spacious boot, and I could bring more passengers – I was often asked to drive men to sites and collect them at the end of the job.

Most of my friends were from the city, but I had some from home and one group from Hospital, a village in Co. Limerick. I had a boyfriend for four and a half years, who I met when I was sixteen, but it had fizzled out by the time I was twenty.

The event of the year in those days was the Hunt Ball, which was always a very glamorous affair. We hardly ever missed it. It was usually held at the Royal George Hotel, and on one occasion we were all still dancing on the footpath and drinking soup at 5 a.m. There was no danger and no alcohol involved.

From time to time my girlfriends and I were asked by lads to go as a partner to a company's annual dinner dance. I enjoyed those events if they were formal. The women wore long dresses and the men wore evening suits which made them look great. I loved making the dress and would copy the latest style, making it with several layers of fabric.

At weekends, most young people dashed off to get the *Limerick Leader* and the *Clare Champion* to see which bands were playing at the local dance halls. I loved the Royal Show-band, with Brendan Boyer singing 'The Hucklebuck', and Eileen Reid and the Cadets, whose hit song was 'I Gave My Wedding Dress Away'. The Beatles were very popular in 1964, especially with 'I Want to Hold Your Hand'.

Céilídhs attracted a different crowd to the showbands. Parents brought their children and taught them to dance sets and waltzes. If you enjoyed Irish music, céilídhs were the best. Even the non-dancers hopped around for 'The Siege of Ennis', which was a simple dance and great fun. I loved dancing so much that I bought a Grundig music player, which I paid for each week. I often danced alone in my flat as we had no radio or television.

Up until 1965, there were no dances during Lent, and we could only eat one main meal and two snacks each day during the six-week period of fasting. It was a church rule, one that I liked as it gave me time to reflect. It required self-discipline and made us question ourselves and ask if we could do things any better. Did we obey all the rules? Or did we even try? Did we use our conscience? Did we do an honest day's work for an honest day's pay?

Lent meant six lonely weeks as we met no boys and I was anxious to settle down. My mother's specification for a husband for me was that he had a farm. Mine was less demanding. I just wanted him to have a soft heart and to be able to dance. If he was funny, sincere, had a personality, was in employment and was tall and handsome, that would be a bonus. On 17 March 1965, in the middle of Lent, I decided to go on another all-night vigil to Lourdes. I had great faith in Our Lady and wanted to pray to meet someone I could fall in love with.

I figured that all the dance halls would be very crowded on the Easter Sunday, after the long period of Lenten abstinence, so I stayed home. In any case, my friends and I preferred the band that was playing on Easter Monday at the Jetland Ballroom, a short distance out from Limerick City. On that night, I was in my usual place in the dance hall, standing on a step beside a pillar. I am five foot two inches tall, so I always stood on the top step to have a view of the men coming to ask us to dance. The band announced that the next dance would be a slow foxtrot.

Then I recognised the tall garda I often saw on traffic duty in Limerick. He never seemed to notice me driving around, even when there was very little traffic. He was about six foot two, and I thought he was very standoffish. He was certainly not on my list of possibilities. Perhaps I considered him to be out of my league.

There were three or four rows of women in front of me. Normally men nodded at or signalled us to come and dance, but he came through the rows of girls, right up to where I was standing. He asked me to dance, then put out his hand to take mine and walked me out onto the floor. I was dumbfounded. It was like what you would see in the movies.

We danced for a while, and I said, 'When did you blow in?', which broke the ice because he looked at me and laughed. When the dance ended, he asked me to have a cup of tea, and I said yes, but in a cool way. We chatted and stayed together until the band began playing again.

When the last dance was announced, he asked to see me home. I had my friends with me, and we all went to my car, which was parked near the door of the ballroom. Everything was just so right about the whole evening, and, in my ena-moured state, I thought he was about twenty-six years old and well up the career ladder.

I asked him to drive because I thought he might not feel comfortable with a woman at the wheel, and he started the car. As we were approaching the exit to the main road, a garda motorcyclist drove in, and the car and the bike collided. The garda was thrown from his motorcycle and was sitting on the ground, holding his knee and obviously in pain.

My handsome garda immediately went to him. There were also two other gardaí in a squad car across from us, beside the ballroom door, who may have seen the crash. I knew they could handle it – it was a garda matter in more ways than one – so I moved over into the driver's seat, went out onto the main road and parked away from it all. I was embarrassed that my car was involved and felt that I was in the midst of the confusion, with everyone crowding out of the dance hall. I did not know if he would be coming in the car with us now or not. I wondered had the accident changed everything and thought to myself that my romance had not lasted too long.

The girls and I waited for another few minutes, and then he came out and we drove into the city centre. We were all very quiet, but he told me his name, John O'Mahony, and that he was from Cork. When saying goodnight at his accommodation in Roxboro Road, he asked to meet me again. I was delighted. I drove my friends home and went to my apartment. I thought back to when he had stopped my car once when he was on point duty, which is when I first noticed him. I had thought he was standoffish, and now he had asked me out.

I felt bad that the accident had happened, and the next day I discussed the incident with Mr Lynch. He told me I had to report it to my insurance and get a solicitor's letter out to John as quickly as possible. I knew it was the right thing to do because of the injured garda. I was full of regret and disappointment – John and I had found lots to chat about in the short time we were together. It was tough luck that we had had the accident.

I had agreed to meet him at a bus stop near his digs that Saturday evening but decided not to go as I did not expect him to be there. However, out of curiosity, I asked one of my friends to go by the bus stop. She did, and he was there. Then I was sorry that I did not go but by then it was too late. We met with the other girls and went for a coffee, and then later we went to the Jetland Ballroom. John was there and came straight over to me. He didn't want to talk about the crash or about the solicitor's letter, and I did not pursue it. He was as lovely as ever, but I was still unsure. I thought of the implications for me as the car owner and wanted to know where I stood, but I was not about to ruin my chances by asking awkward questions. John knew the solicitor's letter was normal procedure and that it had to be sent. As time went by, I discovered no claim was made, so I need not have taken any action.

The whole thing was soon forgotten and from then on we met every day: on my way to work if he was on early duty or afterwards when he was off duty. We used to go to the pictures and then to a dance or for coffee. We could not go to my apartment as my landlady at that time allowed no boyfriends (nor did any others back then).

I could not believe my luck; I simply adored him. It helped that we both came from similar backgrounds and had much in common. I knew that he was educated and that he was a gentleman. He had been a boarder at the Mill Hill Fathers, Freshford, Co. Kilkenny, but he had left because he was lonely and missed home.

From the beginning, John was very committed and serious. Knowing that, I introduced him to my parents. My dad shook hands with him and said, 'This is the first time I've shaken hands with a peeler, and I am only doing it for Angela.' Dad was small in stature compared to John and was looking up at him as he spoke. I was so embarrassed.

My mother practically ignored John and, when he was out of earshot, told me that he was 'only a go-the-road'. A 'go-the-road' was an old term, one Mam used regularly, to describe people with no land. 'What good is he to you? He has no farm.' It was Mam's belief that a woman who had land would have some hope of surviving and rearing a family if her husband did not give her his wages, as she could grow her own produce, just as Mam had done. There was truth in my mother's words that a woman should have some form of independence.

That was the welcome John received when he first met my parents. It was no reflection on him as a person. I believed John was sent to me, following my trip to Lourdes, and I told him so. When he was on night duty in the winter months, especially on frosty nights, I sat in my car nearby so he could sit in from the cold for a few minutes every now and then. I brought a hot-water bottle and a flask of tea that we shared. I wanted to show I cared, but I could not say it in words.

To me, he was perfect. He spoke beautifully and was very knowledgeable on history and politics. I loved listening to him. He was funny but genuine. When we met people, he was friendly, and when we attended a party he always sang if asked. As time went by, he began to give me some of his wages to save for him, and that was a real surprise.

After we had been going out a couple of months, having met about fifty times, he told me he was going home to Millstreet, Co. Cork, for his two days off and asked if I would come and collect him. I wondered if I was actually going to meet his family or if he just wanted a lift back to Limerick. In any case, I took no chances and bought a new suit for the occasion.

He had given me directions to his home, but I missed the turning to his driveway. A local told me I had gone too far, so I turned, and on my way back I saw him at the top of the road. When I got close to the house, I saw his father at the door, popping off his cap jokingly.

John's mother welcomed me. He had told me there were eight in his family: four boys and four girls. One sister worked away from home so I only worried about meeting three. I hoped they would like me as that would be very important. Funny, I was not worried about meeting the younger three brothers.

I caught my breath and settled in and began to take in the surroundings. It was a two-storey farmer's house with very large rooms, literally twice the size of ours. There was a large range in the kitchen so the house was warm. I was a bit thrown when his three sisters arrived together.

I felt the visit went very well. On the journey home, John told me that he had watched my car once when it was parked badly at the railway station in Limerick. He waited for a long time so he could give me a ticket. (Back then, the garda had to meet the driver in person to do so.) However, when he went for his break, I arrived back off the train and drove away, not knowing that a garda had been waiting to fine me. John had been very annoyed to see the car was gone. He then began to look out for it, and he did not have too long to wait. That was when he first noticed me. That threw me a little as I thought he knew me long before that from driving around Limerick several times a day.

Life was wonderful, and I was learning more about John all the time. He told me that he had handed in his resignation as he had decided to go to Australia with a friend from his digs. However, when he wrote to his parents and informed them of his decision, his father came to Limerick to talk him out of it, and he withdrew the letter. That did not sit too well with me – I had marriage in mind. I was disappointed that he was not happy in his job.

I didn't relish telling my mother how serious we were. She was always putting me off marriage, and I am sure her intention was to stall things until I met a farmer. She kept asking me what would happen if John did not hand me his wages after we were married and what would I live on?

She gave us a hard time. John often went to my parents' house, and if he arrived before me he would have to sit there listening to Mam going on about land. He knew that it was the old way and that there was some truth in it. He told me my mother once said to him, 'Sure Angela will be marrying into a farm, and they'll join the two farms together. You have no business here.' I worried that he would get sick of all the talk of land and leave me. I begged Mam to leave us alone or I would stop going home, and she did.

One evening, John and I went out for a drive on the Old

Cork Road near Limerick. We came to a crossroads where it was difficult to know who had the right of way. John did not stop, and a car crashed into us. A veterinary surgeon and his pregnant wife were in the other car. Even though the impact was on John's side, he escaped with only an injury to the forehead, and the other couple and I were uninjured. They were unbelievably kind and understanding at the scene of the accident. I was very concerned for the pregnant woman. We visited them later, and I can still remember her smile and welcome.

I drove John to Barringtons Hospital to be checked. After a short wait in A&E, he was taken into a room to be examined. I was sitting outside on the bench and could hear what was being said. I was totally unprepared for what came next.

'I have to take your details,' the nurse said and asked him what age he was. 'Nineteen,' said John. When I heard that, I thought, *Oh sweet God! I don't believe this!* He was over two years younger than me! My world just fell apart. I wanted to run out, but I was worried that he might have a serious injury. I thought immediately of his parents and what they must have thought of me when I called to their house.

When John came out, he was calm and relaxed and noticed nothing, but I told him that we could not continue to see each other. He needed to be with friends his own age, and he was to go and enjoy life. Otherwise, he would have regrets. We could not meet again. He did not seem to know what I was fussing about.

I was heartbroken when I dropped him off at his accommodation. I worked out that he must have sat his Leaving Certificate and gone straight into Templemore Garda Training

College. He would have only just arrived in Limerick when I met him. I stayed up all that night, consoling myself that it was the right thing to do and decided to get on with my life. I did not hear from him for a couple of days and thought, *Okay, he's gone. He agreed with what I said.*

I was totally engulfed in self-pity. I reminded myself again that he had been too good to be true. I had a few words for Our Lady of Lourdes too. I had never felt that way about anyone before. I enjoyed being with him, especially when I went to his home to work on the farm and when he came to ours to make hay and have tea out in the fields. I asked myself whether I should have parted with him, but I truly believed it would be unfair to tie him down.

To add to my difficulties, Mr Lynch was unhappy in Limerick and began spending more time in Dublin. He told me he was opening an office there. I did not believe it would be to any advantage as there would be more competition in Dublin. Many handymen were getting the smaller contracts, and the large, well-known contractors were all going after the same work. I wondered if he was romantically involved with someone there, as it had come out of the blue, or if he thought a Dublin address would be prestigious.

Then John phoned. As if nothing had happened, he told me he had gone home for his days off. He asked to meet me. I refused, feeling he had not taken heed of what I had said. We finished our call agreeing to be friends. He telephoned again two days later and we had the same conversation. Then we met for coffee. I mentioned his age again, and he told me that it didn't matter. He asked me what difference two years made anyhow. I said, 'It would not matter if you were older. But you are only nineteen, and that is the problem.' However, he kept calling and asking to meet, and I could not resist.

I soon forgot about our age difference, and we got back together. We met every day, often morning and evening, and then he asked me to marry him. We got engaged that August, 1965.

John decided we would celebrate by going to Killarney and then continue to the Puck Fair in Killorglin, Co. Kerry. We would stop by his home on the way to show them the engagement ring. His mother had sent him the price of the ring, and I was glad as that made it extra-special. On the journey to Millstreet, I often opened my handbag to have a peep at it.

When we arrived at his house that evening and showed the ring to his family, his mother asked me why I was not wearing it. I explained that I did not want anything to happen to it. She told me to put it on my finger and that there was no need to be that careful. It never came off after that.

We continued going to dances and to the cinema, usually to see westerns. John loved anything with cowboys in it. He was fascinated by American history, especially the history of the different Indian tribes, and often talked of the Irish who fought in the American wars. I was just in awe of how he could remember all the dates and details of battles. He might talk about Robert Lee one night and the next night it could be the battle of the Little Bighorn. He also knew all the movie stars and could never understand how I mixed them up. (I had only been to the cinema about a dozen times before I met him.) He also loved music, especially Charley Pride, Hank Williams and Merle Haggard, and he sang their songs when we drove around in the car or when people asked him.

With my personal life in excellent shape, I became interested in what was happening about the office in Dublin. I heard that it was going ahead for certain. Soon after it was opened, I was told by the new girl running the Dublin office that I could have a five-day week and annual holidays. I had worked six days a week for six years with no holidays, so the news was life-changing.

At first, the short week was fantastic, but after a couple of Saturdays off I got bored and began dressmaking. I knew Mr Lynch was not out on site as much as before and that he sent his foremen to do inspections. Suppliers were calling for payment, and I had to direct them to Dublin. The new machines were lying idle. No extra work was coming in, despite the expansion.

My colleague in the office and I both felt we needed to act. She went for an interview at a builder's supplier and got the position. Many of the steeplejacks had moved on and had taken building work. Most of the neighbours knew what was happening and were looking out for me.

I was trying to decide what to do when my friend called from Progress International, Shannon Airport, and told me there was a vacancy for a shipping clerk and that I should apply. I went for the interview and was awarded the position. When I gave my notice to Mr Lynch, he asked what was wrong. I told him I did not have enough work and had no direction, that suppliers were not being paid and that I could not face them as I knew them all. I felt I had to leave.

I did not understand him at all. He was oblivious to what was happening to his steeplejacks, to his expensive machinery, to the office and to the customers. He was totally different to the man I once knew and worked for. He sent no one to replace me or to keep the office open. It was a sad day when I left, and sadder still when I passed by weeks later and saw the door wide open. I did not go in. Neighbours told me that everything valuable had been taken and that they had heard the phone ringing for a time afterwards. The office was never used again.

3

Starting Collins Steeplejacks

I enjoyed my new job at Progress International. It was different, the work was easy, and it was stress-free as I had no responsibility. I had no loan on my car, and I received a bus allowance and money from four girls who travelled with me from Limerick to Shannon, so I ended up with the same income. I was still perplexed as to what had happened and was sorry to see Mr Lynch's business end.

In February 1966, John went back to Templemore to do a course that took four weeks. While he was away I became involved with putting on a play for Progress International for the Tops of the Town competition in Limerick. The rehearsals took my mind off John for a while, but I did miss him. I went to Templemore to see him at weekends and brought my parents once. They enjoyed going for the drive and had never seen Templemore, nor had they known about the training college until then.

Though the wedding was five months away, I used the time to design and make my wedding dress. I chose my bridesmaids, designed the dresses and sewed them. I was delighted when all the important things were done and I could spend more time with John when he returned from Templemore. Just as we were very happy, we received the bad news that John was being transferred from William Street garda station in Limerick to Salthill garda station in Galway, which was over sixty miles away. He refused that transfer. His next offer was to Foynes garda station, in Foynes, Co. Limerick, and he was told he had to accept the position even though it was over a half-hour drive from Limerick. That was not what we wanted to hear. It meant we could not see each other as often, and there were extra costs that we had not expected. Worst of all, he had to stay in Foynes and pay for accommodation, and I had to do the same in Limerick. We had one car, so John travelled by bus or took a lift as often as he could, and I drove out on occasion when he could not get to Limerick.

One day, I gave him my car to travel to Foynes for duty. He was to come and pick me up from Mallow Street. I was waiting for him there when a man called to the door. My landlady answered and called me. I came down quickly with rollers in my hair. The man told me, 'Your fiancé had a crash and is in the Regional Hospital. You need to go right away.'

The man had witnessed the accident and had talked with John, who gave him my details and asked him to call to me when passing Limerick. John had been overtaking a car at Clarina Cross outside Limerick when he skidded, and the car turned right around to face backwards, crashing into a car parked across the road. It then careered to the right-hand side into a wall. John was catapulted out of the driver's seat and landed on a box hedge. That hedge saved his life because my car was a complete write-off.

I went into shock. I ran down the steps of my flat and up Mallow Street, down O'Connell Street, along the Crescent, past the Redemptorist Church, out O'Connell Avenue and through Ballinacurra. I kept running until I reached the hospital – a distance of about three miles, crying all the way. I didn't think of calling a taxi or a neighbour.

I ran through the hospital with the rollers dangling off my head, which was not done in those days. I found John, and he looked bad as he had blood running out of his ear and nose and scratches on his face. The nurse told me he looked worse than he was. They had already checked him and had the X-ray results. He was fine. They wanted to keep him in for observation, but John discharged himself. I was very happy that he had not been badly injured and joked with him later that he had written off my dowry.

Losing my car was a setback as our wedding was just three months away. To add to our misfortune, I had downgraded my insurance for the first time from fully comprehensive to third party to save money. With no insurance to cover the cost of replacing the car, we had to buy a second-hand Austin A40, which made a dent in our savings. We did not foresee the extra cost. We had rented a two-bedroom flat in Thomas Street in addition to John's accommodation in Foynes, as we needed a base to be together after we got married. (Couples could not live together before marriage back then.)

John and I were married the following August, in 1966, after knowing each other for a year and four months. On the eve of the wedding, John booked into a B&B beside St Joseph's Church in Limerick as that was the church in which we were getting married. Tradition says that the bride is not supposed to see the groom the night before the wedding, but we ignored that, and John, my cousin Catherine and I talked until 1.30 a.m. Catherine was only thirteen – she was one of my brides-maids, with John's sister Mary, who was the same age.

My parents and my brother Sean travelled from Kilkishen – Sean dropped Dad to my flat, and Mam went with Sean to the church. My brother Michael, his wife Patsy and their son Ronan drove from Shannon. My brother Paddy and his wife Mary came from Sixmilebridge with their children, Brid, Phil (my flower girl) and Patrick. My brother Martin and his wife Moira attended from London, and John's family, along with aunts, uncles and cousins, arrived from Millstreet on a hired bus. My sisters-in-law helped me get ready.

Father Sheedy, our dear friend, married us in the church on the street where I had worked for so many years. The ceremony is as clear to me today as it was that day in 1966.

We held the reception at the Lakeside Hotel in Killaloe, Co. Clare, fourteen miles from Limerick. The view was lovely, and the hotel was also the cheapest we could find. Mr Lynch attended and gave a speech. We were glad to see him, but I could tell he was a different man. From our conversation, I gathered that the investors had left and that he was managing with just a few lads in Dublin.

The wedding breakfast went off well. The speeches were short and courteous, as most country people were shy and left that part to the priest. My father was the exception: he was delighted to stand up, and he talked about me being as handy as a man on the farm, that I had stood on a tram of hay when I was nine years old, that I could follow a horse, plough a field and so on. I marvelled as to why he was harping on about all the work, but, looking back now, it was sweet of him to be so proud. He welcomed John into the family, but then he began to cry and sat down. My mother was quiet and showed no emotion. I knew she worried about my future, and that would not change. I was lonely leaving them as we were always close.

John and I planned to go to London for two weeks and to spend the first one on our own and the second with Martin and Moira. On arrival, I developed a nasty cold. It was awful being in a B&B without a hot drink. When Martin and Moira arrived back we were glad to leave and be with them where we felt right at home. They showed us all the wonderful sights of London.

When John and I arrived home from our honeymoon, he went to Foynes, and I stayed in Limerick, as I was still working in Shannon. For months I travelled out to him. We sat in the car as the rules were the same: he had a landlady, and no girlfriends or wives were allowed. That was difficult, and all the driving was tiring and expensive.

My life was not what I had envisaged a garda's wife's life would be like. There was no sign of him being sent back to Limerick and no house for rent near his station. He often came in to our flat in Limerick but when there was an emergency he had to return. Then he was told he had to live within a certain radius of his station.

One evening, on the way home from work, I was driving along the Ennis Road when I saw Chief Superintendent Flynn of An Garda Síochána, Limerick Division, out in his garden trimming flowers. I knew from John that if he were to get a transfer he would have to go through the normal channels, and that would take a long time with no guarantee of success. Though I was married to John and a garda's wife, I could, as a civilian, approach Chief Superintendent Flynn about getting John transferred to Limerick.

I acted on instinct. I stopped the car and jumped over the low wall outside his house, apologising for my intrusion. I told him my story, about incurring enormous costs due to paying accommodation in two places and having to travel to meet. I was respectful, but I was upset and let him know that. I told him that I didn't think marriage to a garda should be so complicated. I was unstoppable until I had said my piece.

For a minute, I thought he would tell me to clear off, but instead he listened attentively. He told me I should do like other gardas' wives and move to where my husband was stationed, but I told him there was no house to rent there and that John had searched for weeks. He was a stern-looking man, but he was sympathetic, and I was amazed at his patience. He told me he would look into it and see where there was an opening for a garda nearer to Limerick. He told me to phone his office the next day and speak to his clerk, Pat Kearney, who would have news for me.

I thanked him so much that I almost fell back out over the wall when leaving. I called Pat the following day, and he told me there was a garda retiring from Caherconlish garda station, which was about ten miles from Limerick on a direct road, and that there was a small house vacant at a reasonable rent. He told me that in two weeks John would be transferred there. I called John and gave him the brilliant news.

We longed for the time to pass so that we could be together in a home of our own. The house on Caherconlish Main Street had a tiny hall, a kitchen/sitting room with a fire and a small bathroom on the ground floor and one upstairs bedroom, which was divided in two. It had no hot water or heating, but that was the case in most homes back then. It did have a bath, which was exciting as we had never had one before, and I boiled saucepans of water to use it. Our landlady lived next door, and we became good friends.

We adjusted quickly to our new house and to married life. I was twenty-three years old, and John was only twenty-one. We went to the movies occasionally, and smoked a little, as it was fashionable in those days. I set about looking for something to do in the evenings and weekends to make extra money. I loved earning extra cash – and spending it. I bought a knitting machine and did work for friends but wanted it to be a real business. I went to Limerick and inquired about renting a shop where I could sell my work and do alterations.

I found the drive from Caherconlish through Limerick City out to Shannon every morning and evening a waste of time and thought about getting a position nearer home. I even thought of renting a large house, renovating it and renting out rooms or doing B&B. I had savings from my years of working and money from my car accident, so we were in a strong financial position to rent, buy or start a business. When John was off duty he went to a couple of auctions to check prices and so we had an idea of what we needed.

About this time, I was very ill and was upstairs in bed when John came up to tell me that Mr Lynch had died suddenly. He had a heart attack while driving in Dublin and did not survive it. He was only about fifty years old, with no known previous illness. We didn't believe the news at first as he was never ill during the entire time I knew him. He had attended our wedding only a couple of months before. The news of his passing was a terrible shock. In the back of my mind, I had hoped that one day he would return to Limerick and start his business again. I thought of how things could have been different. It was surreal to think so much could have happened in a matter of months.

I thought back on the six years I had worked for him. When I was sixteen, he trusted me to take care of his office and extend his business. He was a friend and always looked out for me, gave praise and recognised any extra effort that I made. He helped employees with loans and allowed them to pay him back when they were able. I was glad his mother had predeceased him as he was an only child. He had visited her often at home in Kerry.

Over the following weeks, I remembered how much I loved the steeplejack business and how much I had enjoyed the work. The trade of the steeplejack came about when industrial chimneys appeared in the landscape (mainly in the heavily industrialised parts of the UK). Sailors saw a way to remain on land, at home with their families. These men already had a head for heights from climbing ships' masts and knew they could apply that skill on land as well as they had done at sea. They designed short vertical ladders that fit into each other, allowing them to access the sides and tops of any type of building.

Steeplejacks could demolish a chimney stack, gold-leaf a church cross, erect a steel chimney or build or knock down a brick one, do plasterwork or change an aircraft warning light a few hundred feet in the air – all in a matter of hours, saving money on the hire, transportation, erection and dismantling of scaffolding. They could carry out any task at any height at little cost and could reach places that cranes could not access. They could lift heavy items into position with a tirfir (a lever-operated hoist) and could winch a seat or cradle to allow a couple of them to work together, cleaning windows or carrying out repairs, and then to scale back down to ground level.

I knew that despite the losses incurred during bad weather, one could make an excellent living from the steeplejack trade. I had gained a lot of knowledge from my time in that business and knew good steeplejacks. And I needed the challenge. So I decided to start my own steeplejack business. If it did not work out, we could live on John's wages – a fact that gave me comfort. I was glad of his secure government job which allowed me to take the risk.

I gave my notice to Progress International. I was sad to be leaving as the managers were very good and I had made many friends there. However, once the decision was taken, I put all my efforts into the future, telling myself that I would succeed. I approached one of the local steeplejacks to be a partner, and he agreed. I prepared the letterheads with his surname and my maiden name, Collins. While my married name was O'Mahony, I felt that it was important to dissociate myself from John's job as a garda. We thought that the head of An Garda Síochána might not welcome wives being in business, which might interfere with a garda performing his duty. By using my name it would ensure that John kept a low profile. There was some confusion because most people in Caherconlish knew me as O'Mahony. When our children arrived, the confusion continued. John ended up being called 'Mr Collins' – it didn't bother him. When I started calling myself 'Collins O'Mahony', that eased the confusion.

I began advertising and bought a second car for the partner. I wrote letters to customers advising them I had opened my own steeplejack company. Then I went out on the road, travelling countrywide in search of work.

Soon after starting, I found that the partnership was not working. My business partner did not want to be away from his young family and could only do local work. It was a real setback that took time to get over. I looked for another experienced steeplejack to be my partner and approached a brother-in-law of Mr Lynch. I changed the stationery to include his name and mine. My first failure cost me money, but now I felt I had made the correct choice.

I had not. It soon became clear that my new partner was not happy either. He told me that he was not interested in the hassle of meetings, worrying about insurance costs or looking over accounts – he had enough worries providing for his large family. He only wanted to work as an employee and not as a director. I wanted him to stay; like the last partner, he was a very good steeplejack. I agreed with his terms, and he became a foreman. He was very experienced and willing to travel, and those men were hard to find.

I now needed another director, but after two failures I

began to doubt myself and was disheartened and embarrassed. I decided I would go it alone. I changed the name of the company to Collins Steeplejacks and printed up new letterheads for a third and last time. I worried about the confusion for customers, but after a couple of weeks, I got accustomed to being alone and began to realise that there were benefits. If I made mistakes, I had only myself to blame and no one else would know about them. I began to feel good and liberated. The experience toughened me and taught me patience and perseverance.

At first I was frightened and wondered if I would be taken seriously in a man's world, but when I advertised for steeplejacks I received many inquiries. I hired two, including one from Calgary, Canada. He had great ideas, told me about different materials and showed me new methods of doing repairs to brick chimneys. I also approached another brother-in-law of Mr Lynch to join us, as he, like his brother, was a very experienced steeplejack. With his arrival I had a skilled workforce. And, as well as being skilled, they were very kind and looked out for me.

The only downside was that I had to leave my new husband to be on the road canvassing for work, day and night. I brought my files and typewriter with me and typed quotations in my bedroom when I was in digs, in my car or on site as needed. I did not go to the pub, and getting my work done was a great use of time as there was no television in B&Bs back then. My challenge was getting potential customers to know about me, and I realised that I would have to spend money on mailing lists. Even though each circular had to be typed individually, I knew I had to do it.

My savings were dwindling due to past mistakes and the expenditure of starting up the business. I knew that renting a house was not sensible, and we wanted our own home, so we began to look around and saw one for sale further up the street. The price was £2,000, and, since John was a garda, the mortgage was passed right away. Because it was on the same street I did not have to change address.

We had three bedrooms, a fine bathroom and a sitting room/kitchen. It was well decorated and had central heating. The extra rooms meant that we could accommodate steeplejacks and save paying their B&B costs when they were working in the Limerick area. We moved in the summer of 1967 and did the decorating ourselves. We travelled to Dockrells on South Great George's Street in Dublin to buy the flock wallpaper I had seen in the movies. I made matching curtains, bedspreads and linen baskets. I must have been mad to make work for myself, but I have always thoroughly enjoyed DIY. A coal fire heated the water, and it was nice to have a proper bathroom for the first time. We were in a happy place.

There was one drawback to the house. It was directly across the road from a very popular and noisy public house. When bands came, they often left at 4.30 a.m., and the revellers talked in groups outside our window so it was hard to sleep. That was something we did not think of before buying.

I heard there were electric washing machines coming on the market and had saved Green Shield stamps, so I used them to get a twin tub. We drove to the Robinhood Industrial Estate in Dublin to collect it. That was the greatest asset to me and to all women as up to then we had to boil whites and wash by hand. John did no housework, the same as most men of his time, but I did not mind. I loved work and was content to see him sitting enjoying television.

Back in the 1960s, work was scarce and wages were low, especially in the country, but there were plenty of opportunities when industries started up in Shannon and Limerick. I asked John's sisters, Breda and Nora, if they wanted to come to live with us and seek work in Limerick. When they came, they found well-paid positions as expected, and we had fun while they were with us. Once settled, they found their own accommodation. Soon after, Nora moved with her employers to the UK. Breda remained working in Co. Limerick and later went into business.

After John's sisters left, my parents began to visit regularly. They loved the comforts of our modern home, especially the television and *The Riordans*, which came on air about 1965. My father often enjoyed a pint in the pub across the road. Then one day my mother told me she was lonesome going home and asked if they could stay. That touched my heart, so I asked John if he minded, and, as expected, he had no problem with them moving in permanently.

John's parents visited but could not stay for long as they had their own young family and farm to take care of. Both sets of parents got on well and had plenty to talk about as they were all from farming backgrounds.

After almost fourteen months of marriage, with our own house and the business started, I was delighted to become pregnant. I suffered from morning sickness, and it was especially uncomfortable while driving the men to jobs on Monday mornings. We travelled many miles, often as far as Tipperary, Sligo and Donegal, and I returned for them again on Fridays if I didn't stay on site.

The steeplejacks were very compassionate and kind to me. I often had to stop on the journey and get out of the car, and I remember once when it was raining one of them got out and put his coat around me. I know I embarrassed them as it was very unusual to see a pregnant woman steeplejack in that situation.

I had to be on the road to keep the company going. I was getting no major contracts, and I wanted things to happen quickly. So I had to travel. I enjoyed the personal contact with customers, but it was very time-consuming because we worked all over Ireland. I did not always have enough work to keep steeplejacks in full-time employment and often had no money to pay wages when the weather was bad. I was confident the business would grow, but in lean times I was glad of the security of John's garda position.

In March 1968, six months pregnant, I was working on a stone-pointing contract on a church in Kinsale, Co. Cork, with two other steeplejacks. John phoned me in the B&B to tell me that a researcher at *The Late Late Show* had phoned the garda station, inviting me to be a guest on the show that weekend. We concluded that it was a prank and decided to ignore it. The following week, there was another call, and we came to the same conclusion. But then I began wondering. What if it were true? Not wanting to look foolish while making a call from the village, I went to Limerick to a public phone box in Thomondgate, and before dialling I put lots of coins in the box so I would not be cut off.

I was stunned when I talked to the researcher to find that I was indeed invited, and plans were made there and then for the following Saturday night. It was arranged that Limerick cameraman Eamonn O'Connor would take a video of me climbing in Kinsale to be shown on the night. I mentioned I was pregnant, which was no problem.

I could not believe my luck. At first I thought Gay Byrne would interview me in the audience, which would have been wonderful, but then I was informed that I was to be interviewed on stage. This was a once-in-a-lifetime opportunity for me to promote my company. I was extremely nervous, but excited.

John asked for time off to be with me, but he could not be spared. His sergeant told him that he was to be on duty in a nearby village where there was something on. I could not go without him: I was twenty-four years old, six months pregnant, not too familiar with Dublin, especially at night, and I was – and still am – absolutely terrified of public speaking and microphones. Appearing in front of most of Ireland with the likes of Gay Byrne was huge.

RTÉ was the only station, so almost all of Ireland would be watching my first time on television. Our only option was to phone the station and report John sick. Consequently, when the time came to leave for Dublin, John could not come out the front door as he might have been seen but went out the back and through a field, and I picked him up there. We drove on to Dublin with two friends, Nora and Liam Ryan. They stayed with John, who could not come into the studio with me in case the camera pointed to him. I always regretted he could not be there because it was a wonderful experience and because I was less confident on my own.

Journalist Joe MacAnthony met us at the Gresham Hotel on O'Connell Street and brought me to the RTÉ building in Montrose. He took care of me and knew it was a big thing to be on the show. On arriving backstage, I recognised the American actress and comedian Phyllis Diller, seated at the opposite end of a long bench. I recognised her because RTÉ broadcast her comedy show in 1967, and we always watched it. The actor Stanley Baker was there and an Irish lady cuddling a young girl.

There was total silence, which surprised me – it would never happen down the country. I nervously looked along the bench, smiling at everyone there, but got no reaction until I got to Phyllis Diller. She left her seat and came to sit next to me where there was more room. She saw me trembling and began chatting non-stop, which put me at ease. *That's more like it*, I thought to myself. I remember her to this day and what she did for me that night.

She asked me what I was there for, and I told her I was a steeplejack. To my surprise, she told me she would talk about us when she went on. She then put something into her eyes (which I found out years later were contact lenses), telling me that they were so she could not see the audience. She advised me not to look at them either. I was to look only at Gay Byrne and then I would be less nervous. Phyllis was called before me, and when her interview finished she stayed on stage.

Gay Byrne was so delightful and professional in his intro-duction that I felt I was someone important! He introduced me as 'Mrs Angela Collins' while I walked on. He mentioned Collins Steeplejacks over and over and told the viewers what I did for a living. Phyllis Diller joined in, and it was fantastic. She even announced I was six months pregnant and was going to have a baby that coming July, mentioning it just as Gay Byrne showed the film of me climbing up the ladders of the church in Kinsale. I heard an 'Ahh' in the audience as the film showed me climbing with no harness. That was the way we operated – there were no health and safety regulations back in 1968 – and thankfully we never had an accident.

After the show, we were taken into a room where I saw Gay Byrne, his wife Kathleen Watkins, and many faces I recognised from television. I sat dumbfounded, and then Joe MacAnthony escorted me back to meet John and our friends, and we headed home. We ran out of petrol near Roscrea, Co. Tipperary, and had to wake the owner of a petrol station, who gladly came and gave us a tankful and who was very kind to us. He told us he had seen the show.

There was no trouble for John when he returned to work. My appearance on *The Late Late Show* did more for our company than I can put into words. It made us a household name overnight, and I received calls from journalists at local and national newspapers and magazines. Enquiries came flooding in, and orders followed. I had come to know many customers during my six years as Mr Lynch's secretary, and many of them contacted me again soon after the broadcast.

Before I was on *The Late Late Show* it had not been easy to find sufficient qualified steeplejacks in Ireland, but after the show that all changed. Many Irish people working in England wrote to us, wanting to return home. It was a brilliant time, although I was humbled with the new situation because I was recognised on the street for a while afterwards.

An older steeplejack, who I had worked with before, telephoned from Dublin for a position, and I hired him immediately. He told me he was going to buy a new van for himself on hire purchase and would then be able to employ men from Dublin and do work in that area. He would look after sites, deliver men and materials and do inspections. That was of enormous help, especially in my situation. He only wanted the deposit from me, and he would look after the monthly payments, with mileage allowance. Others offered to do the same. I wondered was I taking on too much, as ultimately I would be responsible for the debt, and I questioned what would happen if we had no work or if we had bad weather for a long period of time, but I went ahead regardless.

Coming towards the end of my pregnancy, I found it hard to rise at 4.30 a.m. and travel to collect steeplejacks, often fifty or sixty miles away, and be back in Limerick to open the office at 7.30. Steeplejacks arrived from Bantry, Tramore, Dublin and Offaly, as well as the local men from Limerick, Clare and Tipperary.

I often drove the men to the main road, flagged down cars and asked the drivers to give them lifts to their sites. Being a woman, I had a better chance. Then I usually had to drive in a different direction to take another crew to their site. When we had work in a big town, transport was always available, but we were often out in remote areas. The steeplejacks were unbelievably helpful and got lifts whenever they could.

I took on a lot of contracts, had cash-flow problems and was short of transport, but I always assumed that if I applied for a bank loan or for hire purchase I would be refused because I was twenty-five, new in business and had no collateral. (In those days it was thought that women should be minding children and looking after their homes and husbands.)

As the years passed, I got more confident and applied for loans. I know it was due to my appearance on *The Late Late* that I was approved – it had raised my profile. Just being on *The Late Late* opened doors for me. I was looked at as being successful, and a loan was therefore not a problem. It made my life much easier, and I was able to concentrate on looking for work.

I remember once having to collect a large quantity of ropes and ladders at the Christian Brothers in Fermoy, Co. Cork, when a job had been completed. I asked John to help me when he finished his garda duty. He was learning the steeplejack trade, which helped him when typing quotations and doing office work. It was well after midnight when we arrived in Fermoy. I had borrowed a truck from my generous neighbour, Martin O'Connell, who owned a shop and pub across the road. John was driving, and our new foreman, a neighbour and I went.

We were trying to be quiet but made some noise, and the brothers came out in their nightclothes to see what was going on. They were astonished at a pregnant woman handling ladders, especially in the middle of the night, but joined in and helped us load the truck. We were soon on our way to another site that was starting the next morning.

Another evening, I was collecting ladders from Portlaw Tannery, Portlaw, Co. Waterford. The steeplejacks had taken them off the chimney stack and had left them on the ground near the base, along with the ropes. Though eight months pregnant, I was confident I could load them on my own if I took my time, so I set out from Caherconlish to Portlaw. On arrival, I loaded the ladders one by one and divided them evenly on the roof rack. Then I lifted the coil of rope, inch by inch, up over the ladders. Its weight held them in place, but I also tied a rope over the lot and attached it to the front and back bumpers.

I set out for home, pleased with myself. I was hoping to be back in time to get John's supper, but, about twenty miles into my journey, the back tyre of my car went flat and I pulled over to change it. I took the jack out and had just lifted the car when it gave way under the weight of the ladders and tipped forward. The only way to change the wheel now was to undo the ropes, remove the ladders, jack the car up and reload. I was doing that when a large container truck pulled up in front and two men came back to help. They changed the wheel and left, and I was very grateful, but I had to load the ladders and ropes again. I did it at my own pace and set out again on my journey home.

I was nervous, aware that I now had no spare wheel, and I prayed that I would get home without another mishap. However, approaching Cahir, Co. Tipperary, pop went the other tyre. I had to pull over again and face the same task. But this time it was worse, because I had to get the puncture on the spare wheel repaired first, which meant bringing it into the town. I had gone a half mile, rolling my wheel beside me, before I got a lift from a priest and his housekeeper. (I rarely hitched a lift myself before that.) I put my wheel into the boot, and they dropped me into Cahir.

I asked a passer-by about getting my puncture repaired and was directed to a housing estate, where a man worked late, so I walked there, rolling my wheel beside me. I found the man and he fixed it. To add to my misery, I did not have enough money to pay him but promised to send it on. I set out again from the housing estate, walking and rolling the wheel, until I got to the main road. A lorry stopped and gave me a lift, and I popped my wheel up on the back.

I was not looking forward to the task ahead. I unloaded the rope and ladders, fitted the wheel and began my awful task of loading all the gear back again. I was weary and upset, but I took my time and lifted the ladders the same as before and then the rope, inch by inch. When finished, I set out again on my journey, dreading another breakdown. I drove very gently and fervently prayed the car would hold until I reached Caherconlish. Passing through the village of Hospital, I spotted a butcher shop still open and bought meat for our supper from the little money I had.

The tyres lasted the remainder of the journey, and I cannot explain the relief when I arrived outside my door. John was sitting by the fire, and he looked at his watch, indicating his disapproval of my timekeeping. By the time I had prepared the dinner it was 9.30 p.m., three hours later than usual. He had no idea of what I had been through. I was worried about my baby and that I might have done too much lifting. I was twenty-five, an age when we are on top of the world, but that incident tested me and I learned from it. This was men's work.

John applied for two weeks' annual holidays beginning 15 June so he could take me to hospital when the time came. I thought I was due at the end of the month, so for those two weeks I continued working around Easkey and Tubbercurry in Co. Sligo. John came with me on one occasion, and we had my suitcase with us in case of an emergency. The end of June passed, John's holidays ended, and no baby had arrived. He was only back two days when I went into labour and headed to the Marian Nursing Home on O'Connell Avenue, Limerick.

Susan was born on 3 July 1968. Mrs Geoghegan, the owner of the nursing home, and her nurses were brilliant. It was the norm back then to be kept in hospital for five days. I asked John to bring in the post and the list of phone calls, and I dealt with them all. Like all the other babies, Susan was kept in the nursery and only brought to me when visitors came. When I went home, all my work was up to date, and I could spend more time with our new baby. I loved being a mother and wished I could stay with her, but it was not possible because of the business. I employed a lady to mind her from Monday to Friday. Later, I asked John's sister Breda if she would work with us, and she accepted. It was wonderful to have family with us again.

John would not change nappies. He believed that this was my job and never left me in any doubt about it either. I did not believe that he, or most men, would have the patience or skill to take care of a new baby anyway. He would have nothing to do with housework or cooking. In marriage, we promised to love, honour and obey, and that is what I did. He asked for his coffee to be brought to him, and I brought it willingly. He did not shop, so when he wanted a suit of clothes or shoes, I brought three suits for him to try on. I did not have to pay for them until he decided on the one he wanted. I did the same with shoes and shirts, and trimmed his hair also. It was ingrained in us that it was a woman's responsibility to look after her husband and to keep him in happy mode, as well as minding children and keeping the home. Of course, after marriage and with our first baby I wanted to do everything myself anyhow.

One evening, when Susan was five months old, we were on the road from Millstreet, returning from a visit to John's parents. I was in the passenger seat, and Susan was on my lap. Breda was sitting in the back seat behind me. It was 6.30 p.m. on 18 December 1968. A lorry had reversed from a farmer's gate, blocking the road completely. It had no luminous strip, and its headlights were facing towards the driveway of the farm, its back lights stuck in the opposite ditch. We saw nothing until it was too late. I remember shouting to John, then I dropped Susan to my feet. Breda and I were both thrown forward on impact, and I went head first through the windscreen. I was badly cut, and blood seemed to be everywhere, even on Susan, which made me think she might be seriously injured. She was distraught and I could not console her. We were lucky that John did not hit the middle of the lorry as we would have driven underneath and been killed.

Traffic soon built up, and everything came to a standstill. People carried Susan and me around the front of the lorry to the Limerick side. John and Breda followed, leaving our belongings and our car embedded in the side of the truck. Instead of having to wait for an ambulance, the driver at the end of the queue turned his car around and drove us to the hospital in Limerick. He stopped at a doctor's house in Charleville, Co. Cork, on the way, and the doctor and his wife came out and took Susan into the surgery to examine her. She was still crying uncontrollably. I knew John and Breda were fine as they were both talking. I did not feel any pain but soon was drifting in and out of consciousness due to the loss of blood.

The waiting was horrendous. Then the doctor and his wife came out with Susan, and I heard him say, 'The baby is fine.' I cannot put into words the joy I felt because there are none. He said he would phone ahead to the hospital. As we drove there, I felt my lips and face swelling and my teeth becoming distorted. Every part of my head felt huge. When we reached the hospital, they were straight out with a stretcher and took me to theatre. Susan, John and Breda were taken for examination.

The surgeon stitched my face without an anaesthetic, which was a terrible experience. He told me he could give me nothing to ease the pain because of the shock. I tried to bear it and be nice, but that soon changed, and I had to be held down so he could continue. I was not happy and let them know about it! During the stitching operation, the surgeon was called upstairs to a seriously ill twelve-year-old boy who was dying, so I soon realised how lucky I was. A different doctor took over and just stitched the wounds to stop the bleeding. He explained that the skin would be puckered and would have to be reopened and stitched again at a later date, which indeed it was. I needed ninety-eight stitches on my face.

I was very sore over the following days and in awful pain with neck and shoulder injuries, but then I began to improve. I asked to go home for Christmas and was discharged on 24 December. That was important as I was looking forward to spending our first Christmas with Susan and having Santa visit. I loved being back in my own bed, and on Christmas Day I cooked the dinner. After just one week I was able to get around without difficulty. We were closed for the holidays, and there is little for steeplejacks to do during the winter months, so it was nice family time despite what had happened.

I went back to the office in the New Year even though I was badly scarred and looked awful. I still had big bulging lips, and my teeth seemed loose, but all miraculously moved back into place without any work having to be done on them. I wondered how I would face anyone as the wounds were difficult to look at, but I became accustomed to the new me, and, as the years passed, most of the scars faded away. Occasionally I fainted for no apparent reason, which did not help my confidence when climbing, but we had no option but to carry on.

I went back to driving and meeting customers, with a scarf across my face to hide the scars, and I always explained about the crash. Over £9,000 was paid out in compensation in my claim, and I received £3,000, which would buy a small house in those days, but nothing compensates for the fear and trauma of an accident.

4

Essco and Radomes

A couple of months later, in early 1969, we were at home in Caherconlish when John took a telephone call from his sergeant. This was not unusual – he often rang to talk to John or to get us to give a message to the other senior garda. I knew John was not that happy being a garda in the country, but I did not realise that he had plans to resign and join me in the business. He was just waiting for the opportunity. It came for him that evening with the ringing of the phone.

The sergeant asked him about some task that had been done in the station by another person and wanted John to confirm what had happened. John would not say; neither did he want to receive calls to our home when off duty. He saw his chance to leave An Garda Síochána and told the sergeant there and then that he was resigning and would put it in writing that evening. He then casually came into the kitchen and told me that he had left.

I was shocked and worried as I was not fully recovered, and I depended (psychologically at least) on the security of his wages. John's sergeant contacted him the following morning, stunned by his reaction, but John was not for changing, and he resigned from An Garda Síochána. The pressure was now on Collins Steeplejacks to succeed. John and I began working together and were able to put in long hours because we were no longer restricted by his garda duty. He was excellent with customers and loved his new life. I soon realised that he had made the right decision.

When canvassing for work, as Managing Director, I dressed in a smart suit, but if there was manual work and the contract was short, I would dress in men's clothing, and John and I would do it. No one ever noticed. I would move away if anyone approached us and would let John answer questions.

Meanwhile, my father surprised us by telling me that he had made a will, leaving me the home and farm and that they were expecting me to look after them, which I would have done anyhow, being their only daughter. I had never dwelt on the idea of who would get the farm, as it was the custom for a son to inherit.

Dad appointed me as executor and made provision for my brothers. These legal matters were new to me, but Dad kept saying, 'One should have one's affairs in order' so that there would be no difficulties in the event of his untimely death. I remember whenever I brought him to town he pointed to the building where the document was kept. It was more responsibility, which I did not need at that time.

Now that John was working with me, we needed more work, so we expanded into Northern Ireland. I was very wary when we opened an office on Listooder Road, Ballynahinch, Co. Down, in 1969, because the Troubles had started, but I needed an address in the North to win contracts. We completed our first contract on Portrush church on 12 July 1969, during the marching season. Before setting up in the North, we knew nothing of the fighting between Catholics and Protestants. We were young and dealing with our own lives down south and were not interested in politics. As more contracts came in, we travelled to the North a great deal and often came upon protests. One evening, on our way home, we heard Bernadette Devlin delivering a speech to a large crowd, and further on Ian Paisley was doing the same. It was only when we saw them, and listened, that we heard the different views and understood the suffering and violence that was happening.

We got to know the different areas and customs and saw armed British soldiers on every street in every town we travelled through. We were often pulled over. A few years went by, and the Troubles got worse. We felt unsafe and closed the office. I remember one very bad day when we were working on a contract in Enniskillen, Co. Fermanagh. Our men were with the rector when a bomb went off in the town, killing and maiming many. We phoned the Reverend to convey our condolences, and it was one of the most difficult calls I ever made. We completed our contract for him, but it was one we will never forget.

John was not happy living in Caherconlish after he resigned from An Garda Síochána. We had made many friends and had settled in well there, but we were ten miles out from Limerick City, and moving back into town would save us both time and money. It would also be easier to collect men and materials. We looked around and found a house in Rathuard, Ballysheedy, on the south side of Limerick – five minutes out from the city. The detached house had four bedrooms and was very private. The price was under £4,000, so we bought it. We moved in the spring of 1969, and we all settled in: John, me, my parents, Breda and Susan.

I got central heating installed, and that made it very comfortable. Then the DIY began. I had timber cut in Limerick to make headboards, lockers and linen baskets, and John and I assembled them. I built wardrobes into the alcoves in the bedrooms and loved the end result. Then we went further and fitted foam covered with leatherette to the backs of the doors as I had seen done in the films. Before long, the new home was ready.

We went on with our lives, and no contract was too big or too small no matter where in the country it was. We even travelled to the Aran Islands, transporting our ladders by boat. It was the first time I saw animals being hoisted and loaded onto boats to be transported to the mainland. The experience of working on the island and seeing its beauty made it more of a holiday than work.

Soon after our return there was a terrible storm, and extensive damage was done around the country. The spire of the Catholic church in Kenmare, Co. Kerry, did not escape. The cross was struck by lightning and tilted over. It was liable to fall through the roof at any moment. The Venerable Archdeacon called and told us that he had a helicopter looking over the damage but that they could not do any repairs. I told him we had experience of removing crosses and could get to him and be on the top of the spire in five or six hours and that we would have the cross secured in a day. I could tell he was dubious that it could be done, but he gave me the order anyhow.

I contacted the steeplejacks nearest to Kenmare and they went with their ladders right away. They rigged up the necessary equipment, tirfirs and winches, and made the cross safe. Once it was secure, they erected poles across the pinnacle of the spire to anchor it and take the weight. The very next morning, we took loose stones off and secured them. We marked each one and placed them on top while we lowered the cross to the ground and sent it for repairs. Once refurbished, we were ready to fit it back together with the stones, and left the entire structure in perfect order and waterproof.

The Archdeacon asked if I could be up on the spire for the final stages. They were taking a photograph to put in the parish history book. On my journey home that day, I thought being photographed for the Kenmare parish records was far from my life growing up in Enagh. I felt undeserving.

Not all our contracts ended happily. On one occasion we were subcontracted to carry out major works. We had six men working for almost two months and asked the contractor for progress payments but received none. We felt we could not leave the work unfinished as that would have affected our reputation and the customer would not have been impressed. Our solicitor issued a garnishee order, which, in layman's terms, asks that the money be held until the issues are resolved, but the customer had already paid the main contractor. The contractor walked away and did not pay us. He moved address so we could not locate him despite making many inquiries. We heard later that he had changed his company name, and people told us he had gone out of business. We were out of pocket and ended up paying back loans to banks and other creditors for a long time afterwards. We were very grateful to the suppliers who waited. That was our first harsh lesson, and it had serious consequences for us as we were paying a mortgage at the same time.

One evening, years later, when we had long forgotten about losing that huge amount of money, the contractor called me to say he was truly sorry and to ask if I would accept £300 – that was all he could spare. It was a pittance compared to what he owed. We never heard from him again after that payment. We tried not to think about it, and moved on, but it showed the vulnerability of subcontractors who are left unpaid if the main contractor decides to run away or goes bankrupt.

In spite of our bills, we were benefiting from major publicity. We were in *Woman's Way*, *Ireland's Own*, *Woman's Weekly*, *IT Magazine*, *Aspect*, *Enterprise*, *Ireland Today*, *Marketing News*, *Business & Finance*, local community books and magazines, and many other publications, which, in turn, brought letters asking me to give talks at different venues around the country. I spoke once from the altar at a confirmation, which I found difficult (women were not involved that much in the Church), but I felt it was an honour to be up there with the bishop. I enjoyed talking to women at the Irish Countrywomen's Association and similar organisations.

From Donegal to Kerry, local papers wrote about the steeplejacks when they saw them working on the buildings in their town. The local people were intrigued by them working off ropes and using no scaffolding. Our story was in *The Irish Times*, *Irish Independent*, *The Irish Press*, *The Sunday Business Post*, *The Cork Examiner*, *Limerick Leader*, *Clare Champion*, *Evening Echo*, *Roscommon Herald* and many others, both in the Republic of Ireland and in Northern Ireland. Without those articles we would not have survived as we could not afford to buy that type of advertising.

We began to make a profit again and were amazed when we received a contract from Ooms-Ittner in Germany to repair their 1,000-foot chimney stack. Now we were international, and we were stunned to think we could get this kind of work. Soon I was able to buy materials in bulk and to get them at a better price, and the men began keeping stocks at their homes to avoid driving to the office, which allowed us to be competitive and to grow, little by little.

In 1969, I received the most important telephone call of my life. It was from a Mr Carlo Mistretta, an American from Boston, Massachusetts. I was very polite and asked him how I could assist – I put on my best Clare accent! – but I knew from his tone that he thought I was the secretary and wished to speak to a man, preferably the owner. I was afraid that I would upset him if I told him I was the owner or if I asked too many questions. I was very excited as this was our first inquiry from the USA.

Mr Mistretta told me that he had just arrived in Shannon Airport and was looking for a company to install a radome. I didn't know at the time, but I soon found out that a radome was a protective covering for an antenna system and looked like a giant golf ball. Radomes can be seen at almost every airport in the world, protecting antennas from the elements and allowing them to operate normally in all weathers. They are a highly complex combination of extruded aluminium and laminate plastic materials, transparent to microwaves (so there is no significant transmission loss), and are used for radar, satellite systems, radio astronomy antennas and space research systems throughout the world.

At the time of that phone call, I had no idea what would be involved, but I knew I wanted to work with Mr Mistretta. I asked gently what he wanted us to do, and he told me that he had drawings. As the conversation progressed, I became a little more informed. He gave me the address of the site, the radar station at Woodcock Hill, near Shannon Airport – an area close to our house and to where Mam and my father's mam came from. I kept trying to impress, but he was having none of it. He asked if someone could meet him, and the time of one o'clock that day was agreed. It was urgent as he had only a few hours in Ireland to get his business done.

I went to Woodcock Hill to check out the site before the meeting. The radar station might have been newly built as I had not known about it and I was acquainted with the area. The building was only about twenty feet high. I had attached significant importance to Mr Mistretta and was terribly nervous about meeting him.

He arrived in due course, and it helped that he looked friendly. I gave the usual explanation about my face. Despite having the wounds reopened and stitched closer together, the scars were still very visible and did not help my confidence, so I dressed well to feel someway confident.

Mr Mistretta told me he was an engineer in the installation department of his company and reported to a Mr Albert Cohen. After introductions and small talk, I tried to convince him that we could do the work. I told him about our company and thought I was doing well until he asked me when Mr Collins would be arriving. I explained that there was no Mr Collins and that I was the representative from the company. I explained it nicely and told him I understood drawings and was familiar with pouring concrete foundations and building work. I then took a chance and told him I was the Managing Director. He continued being courteous, but I knew he wanted to have man talk! He said, 'Oh, what have I got myself involved with now? And a woman at that!'

It would not have mattered what he said to me as I knew that I was actually making inroads. I had references and photographs of work completed and assured him we would give him every support. I inquired if he had drawings, and he began to soften a little. He reluctantly brought them from his briefcase and we looked over them on the hood of the car. The wind almost blew them away.

The drawings of the base plate were clear and easy, and he realised that I understood what he was referring to. I seemed to be asking the right questions – I was trying to find out what he wanted us to do – and I believe he soon forgot I was a woman because he loosened up and began to tell me about the work, and I listened carefully and with interest.

I priced the work, and we were awarded the contract. Little did I know that the meeting would be the start of a lifelong friendship with Carlo Mistretta, his family and his company,

Essco (short for Electronic Space Systems Corporation). After Mr Mistretta left, we began work, laying a concrete base and template on which he was going to assemble his radome on his return.

Soon after the base was completed, the radome arrived by lorry to site, and Mr Mistretta drove up shortly afterwards. We began unpacking the crates to see what a radome looked like. We saw triangular white panels of various sizes, and Mr Mistretta instructed us on how to assemble them and create a base section. We continued fitting panels, layer upon layer, using thousands of bolts, until Ireland's first radome was completed.

I made an Irish stew after work and went home at lunchtime the next day to heat it and bring it to the site, and all enjoyed it. It warmed the workers and helped them to work well into the night. During the contract I invited Mr Mistretta to our house for meals. John and I were only married a couple of years, and I had no experience of entertaining business people, but I cooked plain Irish food and Mr Mistretta seemed pleased. My best was a stuffed pork steak with prawn cocktail starter – a simple enough meal.

Mr Mistretta was a real family man, and we had no shortage of conversation. He had travelled the world, but we were still very comfortable in his company. We were very unworldly and found him fascinating. He talked of his life in America and told us that he went to the supermarket with his wife on Sundays. I was flabbergasted as I never saw men shopping, nor had I heard of shops opening on Sunday. When he talked about giving us installation work, we could not believe our

Climbing a brick chimney in Mullingar with my children, John and
Susan, looking on.

My parents on their wedding day in January 1933. My mother, Mary McNamara, is front left and my father, Martin Collins, front centre.

The earliest surviving photograph of me taken in Ardane, Kilmurry, Co. Clare.

My grandfather, Matthew McNamara, and my aunt Annie, mam's sister, travel by ass and cart from Gallows Hill to visit us in Ardane.

Left: John and me at a dance in the Jetland Ballroom, Ennis Road, Limerick in 1965.

Below: Our wedding photograph, 2 August 1966. *Left to right*: my brothers Michael and Sean, Mam, John, me, Dad and my brothers Paddy and Martin.

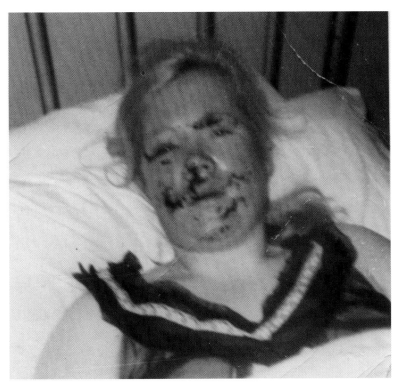

My face, soon after receiving ninety-eight stitches when I was a passenger in a car involved in a crash near Charleville, Co. Cork in 1968.

John signing his resignation from An Garda Síochána.

Minister Tom O'Donnell cutting the ribbon at the opening of the Essco Collins factory in 1976 at Enagh, Kilkishen, Co. Clare. *Left to right*: Tom O'Donnell, Mrs Anna Cohen, Mr Albert Cohen, myself and Dr Harty, Bishop of Killaloe.

Front row (left to right): My husband John, Kieran O'Donnell, me, Fine Gael Minister Tom O'Donnell, Rev. Fitzpatrick PP, Anna Cohen, Albert Cohen, Carlo Mistretta and Jim McInerney. Standing are family, neighbours, politicians and friends. This picture was taken after the opening of the factory in 1976.

Right: Collins Steeplejacks installing Ireland's first radome, at Woodcock Hill, Co. Clare, where we first met the American Company Essco.

Below: A Chinese delegation to Essco Collins Ltd. In the picture are Albert Cohen (*fourth from left*), me (*fourth from right*) and Minister of Industry and Commerce Desmond O'Malley (*third from right*).

Victor Kiam of Remington and me giving a talk at the Irish Management Institute, Dublin, with Feargal Quinn.

Me with John Bruton, then minister for finance, and Peter Coogan, managing director of Bowmaker Bank, after receiving the Bowmaker Award for Irish Industry in 1986.

Winner of the Cork Great Race, 16 June 1985.

Climbing the spire of Kenmare parish church to replace
the cross for Reverend Archdeacon Stritch.

Cleaning a church in Longford.

Outside the Woodcock Hill radome.

Climbing down County Hall, Cork, in 1985.

Me with Jean Kennedy Smith, a former US Ambassador to Ireland and sister of the late John F. Kennedy, when she received her honorary doctorate from HETAC at Dublin Castle.

Me pictured with Taoiseach Albert Reynolds after I received an honorary doctorate from NCEA/HETAC at Dublin Castle.

John and myself with Seamus Mallon, then first deputy minister of Northern Ireland and deputy leader of the Social Democratic and Labour Party, when he received an honorary doctorate from HETAC in Dublin.

Above: Christy O'Connor giving a golf lesson in 1986 at the opening of our nine-hole golf course in Clonlara, Co. Clare.

Left: The Veuve Clicquot Business Woman of the Year Awards in Paris, 2002. I won the award in 1980.

Right: My daughter Martina when she won the World Irish Dancing competition in 1989. She retained her title in 1990.

Below: My family at our fortieth wedding anniversary 2006. *Back row (left to right)*: my daughter Hilda, husband John and son John. *Front row (left to right)*: my daughter Martina holding my granddaughter Kate, my daughter-in-law Fiona holding my granddaughter Karen, my granddaughter Emma, me, my daughter Susan and my son-in-law Seamus Lynch holding my grandson Andy.

My daughter Susan in 2015.

Our grandchildren: Andy Lynch and Karen, Kate and
Emma O'Mahony.

luck. He was interested in how I became Managing Director of my company, and I told him that story.

I explained to him all the different types of work we did, from painting and pointing a small parish church to repairing spires on churches and roofs on factories, hospitals and commercial buildings. I had photographs of us on Electricity Supply Board chimneys, replacing warning lights without any scaffolding and fitting lightning conductors.

One evening, Mr Mistretta asked to use the telephone and called America to speak to his boss, Mr Cohen. He left the door open and knew we could hear in the next room. He told Mr Cohen that the radome had been assembled in less time than he had expected and that he was very pleased. He then told him he would use us on other contracts, especially those coming up in Greece. We loved hearing that as we had given everything during those days to get that exact result. We fell over ourselves with delight, and, once he left, we dashed to the atlas to see where Greece was.

The radome stayed on the concrete base until the weather was calm enough for a crane to lift it over the existing antenna of the radar station. This took three-quarters of an hour. I was on top of the radome with another steeplejack when the crane lifted it into position. Each bolt fit beautifully. The installation was filmed by local RTÉ cameraman Eamonn O'Connor and was on the main evening news. The steeplejacks, John and I were delighted with the publicity.

Mr Mistretta returned to the USA with the promise that he would be in touch. On his next visit to Europe, he stopped off in Ireland and brought us brochures about his products, which explained the benefits of radomes. His company had been formed in 1961 to manufacture metal space frame radomes, and later, in 1965, they increased their activity and designed and developed antenna systems for radio astronomy applications. Their radio telescope systems were installed at the Mackenzie Presbyterian University in São Paulo, Brazil; at the National Radio Astronomy Observatory in Green Bank, West Virginia; and at the Helsinki University of Technology in Finland. They were also at the Onsala Space Observatory in Sweden; the Instituto Geográfico y Catastral in Madrid, Spain; the University of Patras, Greece; and the University of Massachusetts, Amherst. The radio telescope at Amherst was considered to be the most precise in the world.

Mr Mistretta was very familiar with the installation of lightning conductors as they were part of his radome product, and, of course, testing and fixing them was part of our core business. We loved getting orders for them because conductors could be fitted in bad weather. The radome installation contracts came at a very opportune time for us, as many textile and rubber factories were closing down, as were sugar companies. I figured if Mr Mistretta was serious, then we would have work worldwide and John might fulfil his dream of seeing Australia.

Mr Mistretta did indeed keep his promise and hired us for Greece. We all appreciated the opportunity and discussed what was expected from everyone. We realised it was a chance that might never come again. Our steeplejacks wanted the work and travel as much as we did so they were fully behind us. We were so excited, but at the same time our feet remained firmly on the ground. We sent our best climbers who would work long hours, work well and impress Mr Mistretta.

Afterwards, he hired us to work on sites in England, and later he hired us on a continuous basis. He mentioned that he was anxious for Mr Cohen to meet us and said that he was going to build a factory to manufacture radomes somewhere in Europe, most likely in England, Ireland or Scotland. I checked out what would be on offer if he came to Ireland, and on his next visit I told Mr Mistretta about the Industrial Development Authority (IDA) and what would be available to him and his company if they invested in Ireland. I told him I could give them a site on my farm, which I was lucky to still own, which was about ten miles from Shannon Airport.

In spite of the excitement of getting the radome installation contract, I longed for another baby and was delighted when I became pregnant again. Susan was almost two years old. John and I continued to work and travel around the country, but I was very unwell during that pregnancy. I went from nine to fourteen stone and had toxaemia and other complications.

On 3 April 1971, our second child, a boy, was born in the Marian Nursing Home. I was delighted to have a son, and we named him John after his father. He was very underweight, developed yellow jaundice and was very frail for a while. I remember my mother coming to visit us in the hospital. She took out her glasses to get a closer look, which told me something if she needed glasses to see him! She wanted to get him home quickly so we could feed him continuously and put weight on him. She was right: after a couple of weeks, he thrived. I kept him in our room until he was over six months old as he had to be fed every hour. I loved being a mother to John and Susan and wished I could stay home.

One day, when John was a couple of months old, I was out on the lawn when a woman waved to me from across the road. I went to chat to her and invited her to see our baby son. We were new there, and John was away working in Co. Mayo, so it was comforting to see a friendly face. Her name was Mrs Lena Howard, a widow in her late fifties with no children. From then on she came regularly. After a few months, she began to cook, and that helped. Then she began to sleep over and had baby John almost full-time. Mrs Howard became part of our family. She loved children and got on great with my parents and with Breda.

Once again I was able to travel and work as normal. In 1971, I did a climb for Michael Ryan's *Enterprise* television show on RTÉ. They filmed a ten-minute segment on our business, showed our letterhead on screen and explained the work of the steeplejack. I was very nervous as I hated the sound of my own voice, but when I saw the programme I was very pleased. They filmed me on two contracts (a chimney in Tipperary Creamery and at University College Dublin) and then at home in the kitchen with Susan and John. Two of our men were interviewed and were asked what they thought of their boss being a woman. They replied that I was the same as any other boss, and they spoke calmly and confidently and were not at all put off by the cameras.

More work followed, and we were able to offer permanent employment to our men. Then Breda met her future husband and left with him to start their own business. We missed her. I asked John's other sister, Mary, if she would join us in Rathuard. She was a trained typist working in Dublin. She came and lived in and was a tremendous help.

Though busy at work, I worried as to why Mr Cohen had not yet come to Ireland and felt that perhaps he was looking for somewhere else to build his factory and that we might lose out. In December 1972, I decided we had waited long enough and should go to meet him instead. He knew of us from Mr Mistretta, so it seemed right that we should meet.

I told John my plan, and we agreed to travel to America to meet Mr Cohen face to face and put our proposals to him. First we would tell him about the capital grants from the IDA for inward investors and about the training grants for employees, and then we would tell him about the Irish Export Board who would assist in selling the product and who had many offices around the world. Most important, we would tell him about Ireland's low corporation tax. Perhaps he already knew what Ireland had to offer, but I wanted to make sure. We could offer him a site for his factory, close to Shannon and Limerick, at a reasonable price, and we had local knowledge. We would borrow to invest in his factory if that clinched the deal.

John's first cousin, Judy Cremin, and her husband, Frank O'Leary, lived in Toronto. We contacted them about our visit, and they invited us to stay with them. We were delighted and decided not to make an appointment with Mr Cohen as he might refuse, since it was Christmas week. We believed he would be home and would not mind if we called to say hello. We thought our plan was superb.

I called Mr Mistretta to tell him that we were going to Canada to visit John's first cousin and would be travelling via Boston. Since we were going to be in the area, we couldn't not stop off to meet everyone! I booked the tickets and took the discount for staying a second Saturday night, as we might never be in America again. We left our two small children at home with Mam, Mrs Howard and Mary. My brother Michael drove them all to John's parents for Christmas and brought them back home once Santa Claus had been. I will never forget the loneliness and loss of not being able to hold Susan and John at Christmas time, even though I knew they were in safe hands.

When boarding the aeroplane, we met Dermot Hurley, the journalist, and told him the purpose of our visit. Later, an article and photograph appeared in the paper. (I still have a clipping.) I wore a big white fur hat and am sure I looked ridiculous, but I thought I was lovely. The publicity was welcome, but we had only been speculating about getting a factory. There was now pressure on us to deliver.

Mr Mistretta met us at the airport and brought us to the Colonial Inn, a very old and beautiful historic hotel outside Boston, near his workplace. We were so fascinated with the number of channels on the television that we stayed up all night to watch it. We were used to only having one. We were in awe of everything American. The next day, Mr Mistretta took us to his house to meet his wife, Annie, and their two sons, Johnny and David. The following day he drove us to the Essco plant. When we arrived in reception, I was like a fish out of water, but John showed no sign of being nervous. Mr

Mistretta took us to the boardroom, where there was a large oblong table and chairs. I had visualised meeting Mr Cohen in a small room where I could talk to him alone, and I was intimidated in that conference room. I thought of my scars, and my mouth went dry. I was twenty-eight, John twenty-six, and we were very unsure of ourselves.

I knew that Mr Mistretta appreciated our position, because he stayed beside us. Then in came one distinguished man after another until the room was nearly full. I could feel myself blushing as I heard their names. Some were titled doctors and others were professors of this and directors of that. There were at least sixteen men seated around the table. Some we had met before on installations and on their visits to Ireland, others we had chatted to on the phone, but there were some we had never met. They ranged in age from thirty to over seventy. I felt weak when I looked them over and, had John not been there, I would have made a run for it. I felt I would not be able to deliver my message.

John came into his own when the men began discussing the Troubles in Northern Ireland and Ireland's relationship with England, as he could talk for ever on history. I managed to say a few words. I told them that we had carried out many installation contracts in the UK for Mr Mistretta and that we had an excellent relationship with the sales manager in their English office and with all the English customers. It was a relief for the Americans to hear that. The Troubles were constantly being reported in the news worldwide, especially in America. I also told them that I had two brothers who were married and working in England, that England was very good to us and

that we in the south of Ireland were not affected by the bomb-
ings. To my surprise, the conversation flowed and everyone was
very friendly.

While they were all chatting history, I managed to compose
myself. I gathered my wits and reminded myself why I was
there. In my mind, I rehearsed what I was going to say. I knew
I would have to do the talking about the grants and reveal
my plan to Mr Cohen when he came in. I wondered if I had
missed his name when they were introducing everyone and
whether maybe he was already there.

When it was my turn to speak, I told them again that we
were just passing by on our way to visit cousins in Canada, and
that while we were in Boston we wanted to put faces to names.
I am sure they saw through our plan and knew that we were
trying for a factory in Ireland. I launched into my sales pitch
and told them about all the benefits of coming to our country.
One man queried the low corporation-tax rate, but I assured
him that my information was correct. I went on until I had
said it all. The offer of a site was clearly surprising to them, but
no one commented.

I waited anxiously for Mr Cohen to ask a question or even
to present himself, but it did not happen. I knew that many
of that group were part owners and would have an input on
expansion plans anyway, so we were careful not to offend anyone by asking for him.

I was able to relax when the focus shifted from me and the
talk turned to the number of Irish in South Boston. We told
them about our love of western movies, and slowly the mood
lightened. We left the Essco factory, and Mr Mistretta took us

to meet the Cohen family. On arrival, we met Mrs Cohen and discovered that her husband was in Finland. We were devastated at first, reflecting on the cost of travelling purely to meet him. However, we were very happy to meet Mrs Cohen, who was a lovely lady, and her three daughters were very friendly and welcoming. We went out to dinner with her that night, and I fell in the snow, but other than that we had lots to say and the night was not long enough.

The next day, Mr Mistretta arranged with a Mr Croy Hartley to take us to radome sites and later left us off for shopping. I loved that most of all, and, though we had little money, I bought clothes for our baby son, dresses for Susan and some for myself. They were so different, and the prices were reasonable.

We had other meetings and evenings out with various other installation people, and afterwards we went on to have a final meeting with Mr Mistretta, who took us on a tour of the Essco factory. That was the first time we saw a radome being manufactured. The whole process was explained to us, from the moment the extrusions arrived until the radome was completed, which was an experience in itself.

He showed us the testing facility, and we saw a giant antenna being assembled. We met all the workers in each department and the factory manager, whom we knew through our installation work. It was lovely to renew that friendship. When the time came to leave, we thanked everyone for their hospitality and their contracts. Mr Mistretta assured us again that Mr Cohen was going to have a factory in Europe – it was obvious that it was going to be where he got the best offer.

Although we were happy with our visit, I wondered what I would tell the newspaper people when we returned to Ireland. I regretted that I had not made an appointment with Mr Cohen, but nothing could be done about that now. I would have to say that there was no news and face the embarrassment. We had taken a chance, it had not paid off, but the visit had been worthwhile.

Then I decided to lighten up and turned my thoughts to our visit to Toronto and our meeting with John's cousin and her husband. Seeing another country would be a great experience. Judy and John, and their families, had been very close growing up in Millstreet. We left Boston on a Greyhound bus and arrived late at night. Despite the hour, Judy and Frank collected us.

We had a wonderful time in Toronto and met other friends from Kerry, so it was a home away from home, but I missed John and Susan. There was no phone in Millstreet where they were staying – and, sure, John was only a baby anyway. We went visiting and shopping, and the days seemed to pass quickly. Soon it was time to say our goodbyes. Judy and Frank took us to the station, and we travelled back by Greyhound bus from Toronto to New York. We stopped in Buffalo and took in a short tour to Niagara Falls.

In New York, we stayed with John's grand-aunt and met his grand-uncle and other cousins who were in the police force – so John had lots to talk about with them. One cousin told us you could get shot for taking a car space, so that ensured we were on our best behaviour! It was phenomenal to visit New York and to see the main attractions: the Statue of Liberty, the Twin Towers, the Empire State Building and St Patrick's Cathedral. To us it was exciting just to walk the streets. I cannot recall having a camera, but we bought postcards to remind us of our visit.

We returned to Shannon with Aer Lingus, less enthusiastic than when we had left and embarrassed to have no promising news about getting a factory. However, we were very glad to see Susan and John, and I promised myself I would never spend that much time away from them again.

Soon after we arrived home, an invitation came from a researcher on Mike Murphy's radio show for an interview, and I headed to the RTÉ studio in Dublin. The weather conditions were extremely bad and the roads were icy. I had a serious skid near Roscrea and went straight up onto an embankment. The car was left slightly over on its side, and I was afraid of it turning over, so I just sat still.

The radio was on, and I could hear Mike Murphy telling the listeners, 'We were to have Angela the steeplejill here with us this morning, and we called her home and know she has left and must be on the road. We're worried about you, Angela!' He added, 'Please call in if you're out there and tell us you are okay, as we know the roads are treacherous.' I felt helpless. Just then, a couple of men came to my rescue and pulled my car back on the road. No damage was done.

I drove straight to phone RTÉ, but when I got through, *The Mike Murphy Show* had gone off air. Another appointment was arranged, and on that occasion I arrived without mishap and got great publicity for Collins Steeplejacks. I talked about my work in a man's world. Mike was complimentary when talking about our company, and I was delighted to meet him. It was a great opportunity as his show was very popular.

Soon after, I met a business associate who was taking children from the Limerick orphanage at weekends and during holiday time. I thought that was wonderful, as I loved children, and decided to become involved. I went to meet the Reverend Mother, and after we were checked out we were able to foster children. They added a spark to an already full house. We enjoyed going on trips with our bunch of children, and, when I was doing inspections around the country, I brought them with me. Some children stayed for a short time and others for long periods.

Sadly I had to stop that temporary fostering when my father became ill and we found out that he was dying, but I resumed it again years later. Sometimes I questioned whether fostering was more of a hindrance than a help to the children, as they cried leaving the nuns in the orphanage, and then, when leaving us, they were sad and lonely again, and we were the same.

It was about three years since Dad had gone for a pint – there was no one to take him as we all detested alcohol and he was getting senile. Mam often brought him a little whiskey, but he did not seem to notice at the end. He was childlike, and, despite all that had happened, Mam nursed him around the clock, which was very tough. She wanted little assistance except for me to lift him out of and back into bed for washing.

The moment he moved or called she was out of her bed to him as he had lots of nosebleeds. When he was totally incapacitated, I got her help. When Mam or I went to him, he would ask with a smile, 'Who have I?' That was sad, especially for Mam, but he seemed happy in himself and had every comfort.

Then, one day, our GP, Dr O'Flaherty, predicted that death was near, which meant we were able to be in the room praying during his passing, which took place at 11.30 a.m. on 15 March 1973. He had an easy death, he just slipped away, with Mam, Mrs O'Mahony (John's mother, who was visiting us for a week), our dear friend Mrs Howard and me beside him.

We kept really quiet when we heard the rattles of death. Mam nodded at me to keep still and not to make a noise that would delay death and cause extra suffering. She held the candle in his hand and nodded at me to hold it also. We were praying in a low voice and said the Act of Contrition close to his ear.

I said this prayer from my missal, which my brother Martin gave me in 1956: 'Incline thine ear, O Lord, to our prayers, in which we humbly entreat Thy mercy; bring peace and light to the soul of Thy servant Martin and the souls of all Thy servants which Thou has summoned to go forth from this world and bid them all to be numbered with Thy saints. Through our Lord Jesus Christ, Amen.' We said, 'Eternal rest grant to his soul, O Lord, let perpetual light shine upon it, and may he rest in peace. Amen.'

That gave us great comfort, and I felt good to actually see and be part of the end of his life. Mam seemed very strong and surprised us how with much in control she was. She even laid him out. Because we were able to predict the time of death, I could call my brothers so they could make arrangements.

We waked him that night in our house, and all the next day, and then we took him to Kilkishen church. He was buried in Clonlea cemetery with my sister Bridget Anne, his parents and his brothers. We had no horses to carry the coffin as by that time motorised hearses were in, and that was what he wanted.

The following weeks were difficult. I worried about my mother and wondered how Dad's passing would affect her. She would have little to do now. Would she begin a new life and visit family, or find a hobby? John and I decided that we should move house to the opposite side of Limerick – to an area she would find familiar.

We set out to look for a house and soon found one that suited. It was on the main Limerick to Ennis road on the way out to the farm in Kilkishen, which was convenient. It was well back from the road on three-quarters of an acre, with mature trees. The only downside was being on such a busy road, and the danger that meant for our children, but we felt we would get used to it. We bought the house for £14,500. It was within budget, as we had our own to sell, and we got a loan for the balance. By coincidence, it was our bank manager who was the other party bidding against us, and the price went up a little, but we did not know that until we went to him for the mortgage. We moved as quickly as possible, hoping that leaving the memories of my father's death behind in Rathuard would help my mother.

We had grown very fond of Mrs Howard and were delighted that she came along with us. We soon settled in with her and Mary. After unpacking, I vowed I would never move again as it was exactly where we wanted to be. There was a bus stop outside the door so Mam could be independent and go to Limerick whenever she wished. I encouraged her to go to places for the elderly to do crafts for a few hours and make friends. She did go for a short time but then lost interest.

I soon saw some change in her, but that was normal following bereavement and uprooting. My brothers often called with their families on their way to the city, and she loved that. She surprised us on occasion when she helped and was interested in what we were doing. She found the church in Caherdavin and loved to go there. We began fostering again and had two lovely children, and I thought that they would keep her distracted, along with John and Susan. Things continued that way for about six months.

Then, one day, she did not come home. I was very worried and drove around looking for her in all the obvious places. I was beginning to panic when we received a call from the Salesian Sisters in Fernbank, telling us that she had wandered in to them. It was a real surprise as she had never done that before. She told me she wanted to stay there and seemed happy. I could understand that as it was a lovely place. They housed young girls who were going to college and also cared for the elderly. I visited her regularly. We were exceptionally close up to that time. However, in those places, patients always handed up their pension books for their keep, and they would just get a little pocket money back. Mam wanted to keep her pension, which she always had when she stayed with me, so she left the Salesians and returned to us, knowing I would not take any money from her.

Then she developed a fixation about getting into the City

Home in Limerick, which was beside our house and should be free of charge as she had a medical card. She knew many neighbours who were there and she wanted to be with them. Despite numerous attempts, she was unable to secure a place due to my income – it was not enormous back then, and we also had a hefty mortgage and overdraft but, due to publicity, there was a perception that we were rich. We had the name but nothing to back it as we were only seven years in business. I could not get her to forget about the City Home because it hurt her that I would have to pay and that she was not getting her entitlements.

Then, one day, Mrs Howard told me that Mam was missing again and I went looking for her. To my horror, I found her with her suitcase in the middle of the main Limerick to Galway road with the traffic winding around her. I'll never know how she escaped injury. I knew something dreadful was happening. I took her to the GP, and after treatment she was fine for a short while, but she was obsessed about her entitlements and difficult to live with.

She soon asked to leave again, and I got her into a private nursing home in Limerick. She stayed for a couple of years and then she asked to go to a nursing home out in Cratloe near her own childhood home. Cratloe was also nearer to three of my brothers. She was with neighbours there and seemed content, and she gave up on her entitlement to free care. I visited her all the time, and I brought her out for half days and at weekends.

I had her house and farm rented since my parents came to live with me in Caherconlish. Property had little value back then, and it was extra work renting it for small money as the house had no plugs and was old-fashioned. The renting was not successful so eventually it was all left unused. I asked my brothers living locally if they wanted it, but they had their own homes. One brother did take the animals as he had land for them.

I wrote to my brother Sean in England and asked if he would return and buy it for a reasonable sum. I could not sell it on the open market because my dad wanted it kept in the family. Sean preferred to stay in England but kept my offer in mind. He returned a few years later and bought the farm, and then I was able to give my brothers their money according to the will.

It took me years to transfer parts of the land to my brother because the Land Registry was dealing with the owner being a Martin Collins, the seller being a Martin Collins (no relation) and some of the land being owned by a Jack Collins, so all the Collins's names caused confusion, coupled with the fact that my dad had not transferred some of the land to his name.

5

The Telephone Call from Mr Cohen

Finally we received the welcome telephone call from Mr Cohen. I was ecstatic when I heard he was on the line. He was very courteous and chatty, which put me at ease. I spoke slowly, as I had learned from our visit to the US that Americans found it difficult to understand our accents, especially if we talked quickly. Mr Cohen told me he regretted not being home when we visited and gave me the wonderful news that he, Anna and their three daughters were going to visit Ireland.

They stayed for the summer of that year. We knew Mr Cohen was in Ireland to see if he would build his factory there, so we wanted him to see as much of the country as possible. Their visit was so important that John and I ensured that one of us was always available to drive them wherever they wanted to go. We went to the famous Bunratty Banquet and to many of the local restaurants. We took them to Ennis and Limerick, where Mrs Cohen loved to shop. We attended the Galway Races, and took Susan with us. I had never been to the races, so the Cohens were introducing us to new events in our own country. We went with them to Blarney Castle, Co. Cork, and drove around the Ring of Kerry. We visited the Rock of Cashel in Tipperary and the famous Waterford Crystal factory. We travelled to the Burren, Connemara and Co. Mayo. Mrs Cohen, being of Italian extraction, wanted to see Knock Shrine. We went on to Ashford Castle, and from there out to Achill Island. We also took them to Dublin on a couple of occasions. I enjoyed spending time with them, and we could see they adored their three teenage daughters.

When they had seen most of Ireland, I asked Mr Cohen if he had any plans to visit the various government departments and local organisations regarding what offers were available to foreign investors. He had wanted to spend the first few weeks with his family, as they were on holiday, but now he told me to make the arrangements. We were welcomed everywhere we went, and he met with officials at the IDA offices.

Mr Cohen was a shrewd businessman. He talked about an offer he had from England and another from Scotland, making us aware that we were competing. The IDA offered him a grant and highlighted the benefits of coming to Ireland. He seemed delighted with all he heard and was impressed that the Irish Export Board had offices in so many countries, which he would be able to use if he manufactured in Ireland. I also told him about the site on our farm. He visited Kilkishen and was amazed when he stood on the hilltop and looked down at the lakes below. I took him to a law firm in Limerick as we had questions about the transfer of land, planning and timing.

At this time, towards the end of their holiday in Ireland, I was getting really anxious, and I offered to invest in the factory in return for a shareholding. When the time came for them to leave, Mr Cohen was armed with all the information he needed to make the decision. We settled back to work, excited but wondering if he would make such a huge move to build a factory out in the country or whether he would, like most investors, move to an industrial estate where all the services were available.

Mr Cohen called regularly whenever he was on his way to Europe or on his way home. We appreciated the work he gave us on installations but now we had this new challenge of bringing a factory to Ireland. That would be the greatest thing to happen to us, and to bring it to the hill where I was born would be remarkable. It was an anxious and nerve-racking time, waiting on him to decide and knowing that he was looking around for better offers.

Then I received a call from him to say that he was coming back to Ireland and wanted to set up appointments with the IDA again. I was bowled over and did as I was instructed. I met him at 6 a.m. when he arrived from Boston. He did not go to the hotel for a rest but told me drive to Dublin and keep our appointments. After concluding our business, we headed home, and he slept on the journey back.

The next day, he asked to go out to my farm and walked onto the hill again, looked all around and pointed to a spot on the ground with his shoe. He said, 'Angela, this is the place, right here, where we will build our factory.' I remember standing there as he spoke. I remained calm and wanted to tell John but had to wait until I got home. Many prayers were said that evening. Our Lady of Lourdes, Saint Anthony and all the saints were back in favour.

Mr Cohen returned to the USA, leaving me a to-do list. There were no objections to the factory, but getting planning permission in an area with narrow roads and no services was a concern. I received detailed drawings, and our engineer ensured they complied with the local conditions and submitted them for planning approval. Eventually, permission was granted and our worries were over.

I asked builders to tender for the work and finally settled on one. We worked closely with Mr Mistretta during construction and during the recruiting and training of staff. I thoroughly enjoyed that and did it with a very light heart. We applied for grants to the various government departments. I had now gone from being worried to being overexcited.

The steeplejack business was going well as we had many installations, so it seemed that life could not be any better. I was very busy with all the extra work when I received the most devastating phone call to say that Mr Cohen had had a heart attack and was in Massachusetts General Hospital. We were totally shocked and did not know how bad it was but soon learned that he had to have heart surgery. We worried for Anna and their three young daughters, Lynn, Missy and Bambi, who were of an age where they understood what was happening. Health comes before wealth, and we then had a different perspective on life. We were no longer dreaming of having a factory but reflecting on how, in a split second, life changes.

We stayed in constant touch with Mrs Cohen, and I asked my brother Michael if he would go over and visit. Michael worked for Aer Rianta in Shannon and could get cheap air fares. He often went back and forth to Boston to visit friends. He knew the Cohen family and was anxious to go on his own behalf. When he was there, he got a message from Mr Cohen to say we would get our factory. Indeed, he was making plans for the factory while recovering from his heart attack. I often reflect on that message. We truly thought little of it at the time as we felt that a man with a bad heart would be talked out of coming to Ireland and taking on the building of a factory. We were happy to hear he had survived surgery.

Shortly after he was discharged, Mr Cohen telephoned me and said he was travelling to Shannon and that he was proceeding as before. On arrival, he went on planning as if nothing had happened and was more fired up than ever. We, on the other hand, did not want to bring up the subject for fear of causing him stress. To me, a heart attack was a very serious matter. But I went along as before, doing what I was asked to do.

Mr Cohen discussed the name for the company, and we decided on Essco Collins Ltd. Our stake in the joint venture was a four-acre site from the farm and a cash injection, which gave us a shareholding of almost a third. We would do installation work for the American company as well as for the Kilkishen factory whenever possible. We were overjoyed.

The 'turning of the sod' was the first sign of progress. We invited Tom O'Donnell, the Minister for the Gaeltacht (uncle of Kieran O'Donnell, a former TD for Limerick), to mark the occasion. Our parish priest and the local curate blessed the site. Neighbours, family and friends were present. We were a small group, and it was a short ceremony, but for me it was a significant one: the factory was to be built in the exact place where our thatched house had collapsed – the place where my father, my forefathers and I had all been born.

I thought back to those different times and realised how blessed we were. New, wider roads and a public water supply would benefit all. The factory would bring wealth and prosperity to the area. I visualised large container trucks coming to the hill of Enagh, to collect radomes and ship them around the world.

Mr Cohen was full of life and happy with the offer from the Irish government. He knew that we were truly excited with our involvement. One day when he was on site he asked that the stones from the gable of my old house, which was being demolished, be kept and used for the fireplace in the conference room. He told us it would be a conversation piece to break the ice when buyers came for meetings.

The local contractor built the factory, which took almost four months due to changes and weather conditions. Either John or I was on site almost every day. By 1975, the Essco Collins factory was complete. We were soon manufacturing radomes.

The official opening was organised for the following April. We prepared well for the event – Mr and Mrs Cohen were anxious to make it a big celebration, and it was an opportunity to bring customers to see where their radomes were manufactured. When the day arrived, Minister O'Donnell returned to perform the official opening, and the Most Revd Dr Harty, Bishop of Killaloe, blessed the factory, with local clergy. Mr and Mrs Cohen were there, with their family, friends and directors, as were our family, neighbours and staff, and people from the various government organisations – the IDA, Anco, Fás/Solas and the Institute for Industrial Research and Standards. Also present were nuns, priests, friends and customers of Collins Steeplejacks, journalists and the media and representatives from Aer Lingus, suppliers, the builder and all the people who had made it happen.

We had a celebratory dinner at the Limerick Inn Hotel on the night of the opening for over three hundred invited guests. I was enthralled by all the VIPs. Coming from humble beginnings, it was exhilarating for me to be in business with Mr Cohen and with Essco.

One man who attended, Dr Donald Howard Menzel, stands out in my mind. Mr Cohen told us that he worked with his company on many projects and that he was a mathematical genius who, from a very young age, could send messages by Morse code. He had been a lieutenant commander in the US Army and had helped decode enemy messages. He had led expeditions to see solar eclipses and had written many books on the subject. While Mr Menzel was at Harvard, he had written books on UFOs (notably, *UFO: Fact or Fiction* in 1968, in which he stated that there was a natural explanation for all unusual atmospheric phenomena). I was not nervous when he visited as I would not be expected to know about the stars or astronomy. He was very down to earth and spent time with our children.

Mr Cohen spent a great deal of time easing us into our new positions. Whenever he came to Ireland, I went with him to visit the embassies and the offices of the commercial attachés in Dublin. I had never been to these places before and was not accustomed to meeting foreigners, never mind understanding their accents. He told me that it was my job now as Managing Director to go and introduce myself, to get Essco's name out there and to sell radomes.

I plucked up the courage and went with Mr Jim O'Brien, who worked with us at Essco Collins, to meet with Mr Krasilnikov, the Russian Commercial Attaché. He was very generous with vodka, but I could not drink. (I was a Pioneer, meaning I took no alcoholic drink; I was also driving.) I thought it would be rude to refuse, so I poured the vodka into a flowerpot behind us. I wondered afterwards did the plant wither or did it grow to the roof!

On another occasion, Mr Cohen and I went to the American Embassy. Afterwards, we had dinner with Her Excellency Margaret Heckler at her residence in the Phoenix Park. I was amazed at all the security checks on my car and all the guards protecting her. With only three of us at the table, I worried what I was going to talk about all evening. I had no need to be nervous. Mrs Heckler was a lovely lady, and I soon found my tongue. We talked about family, business and normal things, and it turned out to be a pleasant evening.

I also participated in short trade missions. Mr Cohen wanted us to travel on all the Irish trade missions, as the Irish were welcome in every country. The first one, I remember, was to Nigeria. A colleague from Boston met me in Geneva, and we travelled on to Lagos together. The temperature was very high, and, because the lift in the building we were meeting in was out of order that day, we climbed up fifteen floors to make our presentation, then had to carry all our equipment back down again. As far as I can recall, the meeting was not a great success. I felt that our both being women didn't help.

These sales visits were partly funded by the Irish Export Board and were often led by a high-profile government minister. On those trips, orders were usually received. The Export Board set up all the meetings for Irish companies. We found the Irish ambassadors and commercial people most helpful, and we benefited from the use of their offices and local knowledge.

Though I loved these opportunities, I could not take part in many due to my commitments to Collins Steeplejacks, Essco Collins and my young family, so John trained with Essco's salespeople in Boston, and he began to take over. He travelled all over the world with Mr Cohen to meet customers, and, as time went by, we employed more sales personnel.

It may sound wrong, but I often put the companies first and my family second. I would not say I neglected my children, but they had to keep quiet when I was working or on the phone, and if there was a customer about, they kept their distance – often for long periods. I knew they were with family and that they were safe, and I always took the time to explain to them that I had to work and travel on occasion if we were to have any luxuries. I told them how I loved them more than I could say, and we always shed tears. That was a time when I thought I could be everywhere at once, and, of course, some areas were neglected some of the time. Naturally, if there was anything wrong with the children, I dropped everything and stayed with them.

I often thought about missing all the little gurgles and laughter, especially when they were babies. I thought of what I was missing, but, despite the guilt, I knew I could not be a full-time mother. The guilt and the hurt never left. Work always came first. Even when feeding my babies their bottles, I could not sit and enjoy it; instead, I shuffled around, tidying up or reading a file.

In the summer of 1976, a few weeks after the factory opened, John and I were chatting at home and decided to have a third child. John had missed out on being a hands-on dad to our first two children. Susan was eight, and John was five, and they were both in school in Caherdavin.

I was thrilled when I found out I was pregnant. Although it was an easy pregnancy, I had an accident when I was about five months along. I had been in the Burlington Hotel in Dublin and was walking back to my car, taking a shortcut across an open green. While looking behind me, waving goodbye to the group I had just left, I stepped off the foot-path and fell down two feet, landing heavily on my tail end. I was stunned for a moment and in real pain. I knew I had injured myself and was worried about my baby. I stayed there a moment, crying and full of self-pity. I am sure the people passing thought I was drunk, which I was not. I knew I would have to get out of there by myself, as no one was coming to my aid, and I managed to pull myself up and limp to my car. I drove to a shop for painkillers and water and made the journey home. Next day, I went to the doctor who assured me that all was well, but I longed every day to feel movement.

It was a huge relief when baby Martina arrived, healthy, on 15 March 1977. She was born on my father's anniversary, so she brought her name with her. She weighed six pounds seven ounces. It was the same as having a first baby – I loved her and enjoyed being a mother again. I had to spend the normal five days in hospital, but Martina was kept with the other babies in the nursery so I grew bored and asked my secretary and John to bring in the mail and telephone messages every day. The typed letters were brought back for signing. When I went home, all the paperwork was up to date and I was able to spend more time with our new baby.

One Sunday morning in 1977, at about 10 a.m., when Martina was a couple of weeks old, John and I were in bed when we heard cars pulling into our driveway and doors opening and closing. Martina was in our room, and it was a mess, with our clothes everywhere and the usual baby things thrown all over. My mother and Mrs Howard were already downstairs with Susan and John.

I looked out to see three black Mercedes parked outside and counted eleven people, most of whom I knew. They were Russians, and they had driven from Dublin to Limerick to see our baby daughter. They included Mr Krasilnikov, the Commercial Attaché, and his wife; the Russian Ambassador, Mr Anatoli Stepanovich Kaplin; and their friends and minders. One of the men stood out from the others as he was unusually tall.

We went downstairs in our nightwear and invited them in. I thought there was no point getting embarrassed about our kitchen, which was untidy. I wasn't fussy about things and did not mind if the dishwasher was not loaded. They had brought baby gifts, biscuits and caviar, which was new to us. We sat them down and made tea, and soon everyone settled into conversation and it was as if they were family. I brought Martina down and thoroughly enjoyed showing off our bundle of joy.

After a while, the very tall man, whose name was Sergei, asked if he could do anything to help. Susan, who was eight years old at the time, knew that my clothes were thrown around the bed and hanging off doors and chairs and that I was always saying I must hang them up. 'Oh yes, you can help me tidy upstairs,' she told him, and they both went and sorted everything! I didn't notice what was going on, but you can imagine how I felt later when I heard what had happened. Embarrassment would not adequately describe it. I would not ask my mother to do what they did. But the innocence of it was beautiful as Susan single-handedly decided not to waste 200 pounds of manpower when it was offered. We were humbled by their visit and the thought that they had given up their Sunday. We hoped that in time we would get an order.

Around this time, John's sister Mary, who had been living with us since our time in Rathuard, was getting married, and she and her husband T.J. were starting their own business. We were delighted for them, but sad to lose her as she was a wonderful help. With a new baby, Essco Collins, Collins Steeplejacks and no young person to rely on, I was in real need of a nanny. I employed a housekeeper, but she did not stay long because my mother told her to stop making noise.

Then I hired another, and she left when my mother got cross with her also.

During this time, I worked from home, trying to cope with temporary staff, but I felt stressed due to doing housework, lack of sleep and the continuing back pain from my fall in Dublin. I needed back-up. I decided to go on another overnight visit to Lourdes, similar to the ones I had been on before. I wanted to bring my mother with me this time. It would be a new experience for her. When I asked her, she told me she would not go on an aeroplane. I explained that once you were inside it was similar to sitting at home or on a bus, and, if anything did happen, she would be on a pilgrimage – so what better way to go? Eventually she agreed, and I made the arrangements.

The day for boarding arrived and she did not blink an eye. Once in Lourdes, Mam was amazed at the candlelit processions. Seeing the different illnesses and all the invalids saddened her but enlightened her too. On our return home, she improved. She joined in more and helped around the house for a while and seemed interested in the children again. She told those who visited about what she had seen. I prayed she would remain that way and that we could live together as before.

Despite Mam helping and the big change in her, I still needed to employ a young person. I advertised again, hoping that I would find some patient housekeeper who would come and work with me and make an effort with my mother. I had little hope of finding that special person, but I had to try.

It was mere days after our return from the pilgrimage that a young woman in her late twenties called, asking for a job. She had a preference for a hotel position, but she told me that she would work with us for a while. We took to each other right away. Her name was Josie, and she was the person I needed. Nothing bothered her, she was patient and kind, and she loved children. Somehow, she managed to get along with my mother and Mrs Howard. Peace was restored to our home, and life was heavenly again.

Josie told me on her first day that she was not a great cook, but I did not mind. John and I could go to work now in the knowledge that our children would be taken care of. We knew that they were happy, and it was surprising to see the change in them. They even began leaving notes and little gifts for us along the corridor and on our pillows. Josie took care of baby Martina and treated her as her own. When we were going to be back very late she even took all our children to her house by bus and brought them back the next morning.

With the home problems solved, I organised for an X-ray to find out what was causing my persistent back pain. The results showed that I had split my coccyx when I fell in Dublin. I had to have it removed, and I spent many weeks in hospital because the wound got infected. John could only visit once every day. He brought the post and telephone messages, but I was not able to deal with them as before because I mostly had to lie face down. It was a very bad time to be out of work. I was not one to delegate and wanted to know everything that was going on, which was not possible. I had severe pain and was unable to stay on top of things. Recovery was slow, and I could not drive for six weeks.

Eventually I got back on my feet and learned from Essco in the US that they needed a second radome product to meet customer needs and that the research, design and manufacture would be done in Ireland. I think it was because we had cheaper labour rates in Ireland. We applied for and received an enormous research and development grant – money well invested – and we had an inquiry from the French government. We then set about designing the new radome, with assistance from the University of Limerick and Mr Cohen and his experts, who came regularly to see it being manufactured.

Eventually our new product was ready for sale. Made of composite materials, it used updated technology to ensure panel consistency and strength. It was electromagnetically tuned to minimise transmission loss and scattering effects at the specified operating frequency and offered random geometry configuration to optimise electromagnetic performance. It was much thicker than the metal space frame radome and had several layers, hence its name: the 'sandwich radome'. Like our metal space frame radome, this sandwich radome was designed to last for life and required little maintenance. The first one was sent to Sainte-Beaume, Marseilles, France, and it was a perfect match for their antenna.

Having a second product increased our sales enormously. We expanded the English office and had an experienced team at the end of the phone. They visited the factory frequently. Soon after that, we had another pleasant surprise when we were asked to quote to erect a 300-foot tower for Marathon

Oil at Inch, Co. Cork. This was the first time that natural gas had been brought to shore in Ireland. The main contractors hired us as subcontractors, and I did worry, but I was keen to be involved.

We did not disappoint them. We had erected many steel towers, but this was the highest we had ever done. Erecting the tower itself turned out to be a simple task, but cash flow and weather conditions caused us concern. We had given a firm price for the contract, so money was a real worry because we had no control over the weather. The site was very exposed to wind and rain, and we had many hold-ups during the job. I had no clause in the paperwork to safeguard us against severe losses due to wind.

Because of the urgency of the contract we used cranes to lift the top part once it had been assembled on the ground. One time, it was calm on the ground, so I climbed to the top to check conditions and to see if we could do a lift. However, once on top, the wind and rain came so quickly that I found it difficult to climb back down. My hands were frozen in seconds. I could not feel the ladder and had to resort to putting my elbows around the supports to hold on. I began to lose the feeling from my elbows, so I was very lucky to reach the ground safely. I should have called for the steeplejacks to help, but I was too proud and embarrassed because they had told me the winds were too high and I hadn't listened to them – I felt under pressure because the cranes and men were standing idle and costing money. To add to my misery, I had an American engineer with me, and I wondered if he had seen what had happened.

During the Inch contract I stayed mostly in B&Bs near Midleton, Co. Cork, and with John's parents in nearby Millstreet. I spent many days on site, climbing and working. When the weather was mild, we began work at 5 a.m. Most of our steeplejacks knew what to do and didn't need me to show them, but we usually consulted each other and then made decisions together.

Soon after the Marathon Oil contract, we received a major order from the Department of Justice to supply aerials and to install communication towers at garda stations, as well as other orders from the Office of Public Works and the Commissioners of Irish Lights, who ran the lighthouses.

Our steeplejacks were careful and skilled, and we often worked through the night to meet targets. Our office staff and field crew cooperated fully, and even Susan and John, who were about fourteen and eleven years old, were asked to help. When Susan was on holidays she mapped all the areas that had been completed and noted the new orders coming in on the map so we could plan a schedule for steeplejacks to go to those sites. John loved being involved with the lads whenever possible.

We were expanding at a quick pace and we were very busy. It meant I could not sit, have tea and chat as much as before. I had to move into administration because I had so many more men employed, and I missed the old ways and the closeness we used to have with employees and customers. I had mixed emotions about the emerging change of lifestyle, but I knew I could not have it every way. I had to prioritise and spend more time in administration and less on site.

In about 1979, China and Ireland began trade relations, and the two countries signed agreements. Soon after, the first Chinese delegation came to visit Essco Collins and other companies in the Munster region. Mr Cohen and our Chinese director, Mr C. S. Wang, came from Boston to meet with the group. The visitors went through the factory and were very interested in every area of manufacture for our radome. Later, there was a return trade delegation to Beijing, which included Essco Collins and many other Irish firms. Mr Cohen and Mr Wang went, and, thanks to Mr Wang's background and language skills, he was able to move everything along.

To our utmost surprise, our company received its first Chinese order. That was very significant for our factory, and we extended to produce those radomes. We owed much thanks to the Irish Export Board, who were well established in Beijing and who had set up appointments for us. They had expertise and local knowledge, and they knew who were potential buyers.

Alan Dixon was one of the people involved, as he was living in Beijing with his wife, Margaret. We knew him when he worked in Donegal and he had dealings with our company prior to joining the Irish Export Board. We were also very grateful to Desmond O'Malley, Minister for Industry and Commerce, who led the delegation and who worked with us to secure the order.

When the radomes were manufactured and shipped, the Essco engineer, Mr Joe Sangiolo, who was part-owner/director and founder of the American parent company, accompanied John to China to train the Chinese on how to install them. They were there for almost six weeks, and the children and I were very lonely. China seemed so far away back then. I was very lucky to have a wonderful staff to talk to in Margaret Leland, Noreen Slattery and Josie, who I can honestly say were closer than any sisters could be, and Mary and Breda from Essco Collins, who gave me enormous help and who often stayed overnight.

It was hard on John, too, as he missed Susan's confirmation and the wedding of his youngest brother, Donie, to Elizabeth. But it was a brilliant opportunity to earn money and work in China, and sacrifices had to be made. The installations were on pleasant sites, and John and Mr Sangiolo found the Chinese very friendly and helpful.

Soon after John returned from China, the first Chinese Ambassador, Madame Gong Pusheng, came to Ireland. It was a very important occasion when she visited us in Clare. She was aware of the order the Chinese had given us, and she knew we expected many more. One order from such a large country would not justify the investment we had made to expand. When her term was over, she introduced us to her replacement, Mr Xing Zhongxiu. We were delighted as we wanted him to know of our company and our product, and we wanted to pursue more orders. Mr Xing came to our factory. We toured with him and his group and showed them Irish hospitality. We still have a photograph of him in front of the famous Treaty Stone in Limerick.

As each ambassador left, they arranged an evening at the embassy for industrialists and friends to say goodbye and to make the acquaintance of the incoming ambassador. Mr Xing introduced us to his replacement, Mr Zhou Yang, and his wife, and we became very close friends. They visited frequently and stayed often. Once they went shopping to the Limerick market and later cooked dinner at our house for everyone. We enjoyed a boat trip up the river Shannon with them, our friend Liam Ryan (the owner of the boat) and Judge Dermot Kinlen, who was their legal adviser and who nearly always travelled with them.

At the same time as we were manufacturing the radomes for China, Mr Cohen had several Chinese engineers in America doing research for him on solar energy. So Mr Cohen, the Chinese and the Irish were friends and worked well together. We continued making trips to Dublin and China pursuing orders, but nothing was forthcoming.

Mr Cohen made regular trips to Japan in the early 1970s to try to sell radomes but was not very successful. We both went to the Japanese Embassy in Dublin many times, and, after Mr Cohen left, I continued making visits. I was delighted when the Japanese Ambassador to Ireland, Mr Yoshinao Odaka, came with his wife to stay with us. We were entertained by the Wren Boys, a group from Kilkishen who played traditional music and told stories. Martina gave an exhibition of Irish step dancing with some of her friends. I know the Japanese enjoyed the evening. They also enjoyed the golf and, in particular, the Irish night in Bunratty Castle. I still have letters from Mr Odaka. He loved the pints of Guinness and the atmosphere of the singing pubs.

Mr Cohen was very persistent and kept making return visits to Japan. He asked the Japanese office in Dublin to try for an order for radomes for us. In the end, there was a breakthrough, and we received a significant order. It took many years, many trips and an enormous amount of time, but it was worth it when it came.

6

Clonlara and Beyond

One evening, as I was working at my desk, John placed a copy of the *Limerick Leader* in front of me and pointed to the advertisement for an old estate house outside Clonlara, Co. Clare. I asked him why he was showing it to me. He replied casually that he just wanted me to see it. A week or so later, the advertisement reappeared and John showed it to me again. I asked him again what about it, as I was puzzled, and he asked me to just go out and have a look at the property. In order to pacify him, I went. I was positive that I was not moving and would never pack boxes again; nor did I have the slightest interest in a country house. We had lived in Caherdavin for only five years, and Susan and John were in school and had made friends.

We drove to Clonlara and found the property. The house stood on a sixty-eight-acre farm. It had stables, outbuildings, a gate lodge, a little dairy house and a power house, which in the old days provided electricity. There were also several other outbuildings with beautiful stonework. The place had a great energy and we fell in love with it. We had no appointment and just looked around. We could not see the driveway or even where it might have been. There was no sign of life and we could see that it had not been lived in for years. It was a very large, irregular, Tudor-style, five-bay, hip-roofed house, eighteenth-century, with many extensions added over the years. The textures were different, but they all seemed to fit in.

The owner did not live there, but he saw our car at the entrance, drove over and invited us to look around. We went through the farmyard and on to the front door, which was open and creaking in the breeze, so we assumed the place was going to be derelict. The owner told us that it had been vacant for over twenty-five years; however, there was little or no damage. The stairs were in perfect condition even though they were covered in dust and cobwebs. The woodwork was hand-carved and ornate and wound up and around to the many bedrooms. Every room had cornices, there was decorative plasterwork on all the ceilings, and I loved the high old windows with their long thin shutters. The Adam-style marble fireplace in the dining room seemed in great condition despite its years. There were layers of wallpaper on the walls.

We enjoyed exploring as there were so many rooms and alcoves, a wine cellar and a large basement with rooms off it. I saw a huge burner that would take a whole bale of hay to heat the giant radiators. There was lots of wood outside from fallen trees that could be used for firewood.

As we looked out the front windows, the owner pointed to the river Shannon, which circled the land from the direction of Castleconnell, Co. Limerick, passing by the famous historic Angler's Rest pub as it wound its way into Limerick City. He told us that this stretch of the river offered the best salmon fishing in the region. All along the front of the house, wisteria, rhododendron, laurels and azaleas were growing wild – they brought back wonderful memories of the 1940s and 1950s, when we used to cycle around Kilkishen to look at the gentry's houses.

I began to imagine living there and thought of the huge change it would be from the city. We would be leaving all the noise behind, as well as all the danger of the busy road. Though the thought of moving and starting all over again was daunting and exhausting, the decorating and refurbishing would be fun. We knew the house would be heavenly to live in. We went home, delighted with ourselves.

The owner was easy-going and friendly. He was anxious to sell and did not seem to want the price quoted in the paper. We put in a lower bid that evening, and he accepted. When he called his auctioneer the next morning, he was told that there was another interested party. Then the fun began.

The auctioneer called and told us the situation. (I remember clearly it was on a Saturday.) The bidding began, and we continued until the price had almost doubled from the previous evening. It went up by at least £100,000 in two hours. It was chilling just sitting there, taking the calls, making the offers, then waiting and wondering before taking the next call. A hotel owner was bidding against us, but he finally gave in when he realised he was up against mad people.

Details of the purchase were in all the newspapers. The UK *Daily Mirror* sent a photographer from Northern Ireland, and they gave the sale a large write-up as well as about four pages of photographs showing the children and myself on the roof.

That was June 1978. I still have a copy. Once again we were glad of the free publicity, as Collins Steeplejacks was mentioned. It kept the name out there.

We began working out how to find the money to pay for our new home. Our house on the Ennis Road would sell for about €70,000. It was in a great location, and my brother's friend bought it and went into the B&B business. But it provided only a third of what we needed. A short time later, we put everything we owned up for sale, even John's farm in Millstreet, which we had bought from his parents. (We were really glad his brother Tim and his wife Mary purchased it.) We knew we could borrow the rest. We could live in the house just as it was and share it with the many bats and four-legged friends who occupied it. It would be a primitive but unusual experience. That we had no need of a house that size was one of the sensible thoughts that came to me but that was quickly quelled. If we were sensible people, we would have walked away. But we weren't. We were up for the challenge of refurbishing the house, and that took more determination than sense.

And so we moved to Clonlara, Co. Clare. It was John's dream come true. He had always wanted a large house with steps up to the front door and a veranda. Well, he got the veranda. The house had no front steps but we built some at the back. An elderly neighbour showed us where the original driveway had been hidden for a quarter of a century, and when it was dug out it was marvellous and circled the front of the house.

We set about making the place comfortable. We wanted to get a couple of rooms decorated so that people could come to dine with us rather than us going out to eat and leaving our children. I bought 480 rolls of wallpaper from Boyd's in Limerick, which was closing down. They cost very little, and, over the following months, we hung every single roll. I wonder why we did not settle for painting, but to this day I love wallpapering. In the beginning we walked on the timber floors and had to wait a long time for carpet. When the children of overseas customers and those of US staff came on holiday to us, they often helped with decorating, and that kept them busy. With all that help, the place was soon habitable.

I loved the DIY and making cushions, bedspreads and curtains, and I did my sewing in the same room as John and our children so as not to miss out on being with them. It was a very satisfying pastime in the long evenings. In between decorating and working in the office I made wedding dresses and bridesmaid dresses for friends, communion dresses for my daughters and a confirmation outfit for Susan. Others asked me to sew for them as they knew I enjoyed making dresses.

I did not forget the businesses. I was very busy keeping on top of my role as Managing Director of Essco Collins Ltd and Collins Steeplejacks during the day. I worked on files late at night when the children were in bed. Essco Collins paid a handsome dividend that helped enormously with the refurbishing and with our debts.

One day, I received a call to go on *The Late Late Show* with a panel of women. I was delighted and was not as nervous as the first time because I was not going to be interviewed on my own. It was uplifting meeting Gay Byrne again. As usual, he was very professional, and, again, it was great exposure. That appearance led to more newspapers calling and to an invitation for an interview on the Marian Finucane radio show, which was followed by more calls from other journalists for my story. I was delighted that the media was interested in what a woman steeplejack did, and was grateful that I had chosen that career, because as long as the magazines and papers kept writing about us, inquiries kept coming and work followed.

I brought my mother to Clonlara from the nursing home, and when she saw we had land she asked to stay. I saw a great improvement in her. I took a chance and bought hens to remind her of home and thought they would occupy her. She attended to them for a few months but then went downhill and told me to sell them. On another occasion she got annoyed with me because I bought food in bulk. It was convenient for me, but Mam thought it was waste and got cranky. She tried giving it away to anyone who called.

She wanted to leave again, so she went to Kilkishen to my brother Sean and his wife Mary, who had returned from the UK to live on the farm. I thought she would be happy there as the house had been renovated and she would be at home with family and with neighbours, especially the Guinanes, Murnanes, Donnellons, Boyces, McNamaras, Liddys, Stephens and Flemings. But she returned to me again. She began having falls, as she had Ledderhose's Disease on her feet, and soon needed full-time care.

One day, she did a very strange thing. We could not find Martina's clothes. I suspected Mam, but before upsetting her we searched every nook and corner of the house. We were puzzled as to where she could have put them. Though she was nearly eighty years of age, she could outwit all of us. Eventually I asked her where she had put the clothes, but she wouldn't tell me and instead insinuated that maybe someone had taken them. I asked my brothers to call and gently get around her, and, after a long time, she showed where she had hidden them. We were just aghast at her cleverness. She had taken a hammer, driven nails into the inside of her wardrobe and hung all of Martina's clothes in plastic bags on the nails. Then she put her own clothes on hangers in front so we couldn't see them.

After that hullabaloo she asked to leave, and I booked her in to a local nursing home again. Then she appeared to lose the will to live. When I visited, she always told me that she wished God would take her. I was helpless to do anything to cheer her up and it weighed on me as we had been very close up to the time my dad passed away. I missed that companionship, but I realised with great sadness that those times were over and that we faced a long goodbye. Of course, in the meantime, other nice events took place, which kept us going.

Mrs Cohen invited our children over to Boston for a holiday. John was eight years old, and Susan was going on eleven. I sent them via Aer Lingus, and they were met off the plane by the Cohens. It was a valuable experience, and they enjoyed the holiday and the American toys. Then the Cohens sent their daughter Bambi to us. It was a superb opportunity for our children to meet and mix with people of other nationalities.

Sons of customers and Essco staff also came for summer holidays, and one young man visited from Africa and stayed for six months. They loved the country life and helped out on the grounds, pruning shrubs and cutting lawns. I know they enjoyed saving hay and working with the tractor. The daughters of other employees came to us, but, strangely, we never asked them to do any work, we just took them touring. Looking back, I see that we had no equality! With so many living with us, our children had plenty of company, and, though it was an unusually busy house, it worked brilliantly for us. Our pool table brought the young teenagers together and occupied them. It really played its part when foreign buyers dined with us. Some of them could not speak English, but they understood pool, and we often played well into the night trying to get the better of each other. It helped to build friendships despite the language barrier.

In December 1980, soon after we had settled in Clonlara, I received news that I had been chosen as Ireland's First Veuve Clicquot Business Woman of the Year. (The widow Barbe-Nicole Clicquot Ponsardin was the first woman to take over a champagne house, in 1805, and the award has been given in her name ever since.) We attended the presentation at Gilbeys on the Naas Road in Dublin as they were sponsoring the event. They gave us a fantastic day. The Minister for Industry and Commerce, Desmond O'Malley, made the presentation.

As it was the first time the award had been given in Ireland, it was on the main evening news. I was walking into Gilbeys when I was surprised by the voice of Derek Davis of RTÉ Television. He was behind the door, and I turned around to see him with his camera crew. Because of the surprise element, I wasn't nervous in that interview.

As part of the prize, John and I received a trip to Reims in eastern France, the headquarters of the Veuve Clicquot

Champagne group, where a vine was planted to mark the occasion. There was also a bottle of champagne each year on my birthday, which continued for thirty years and the odd year after that. Again, the publicity enhanced our image and was excellent for business.

We always did business during the Essco Collins–Collins Steeplejacks Christmas party, which, strangely, was usually held around the beginning of February each year because it was not always possible to get people together any other time. One year, Mr Cohen asked me to invite Albert Reynolds, Minister for Industry and Commerce, and Mr Delaney, a senior member of the Irish Export Board, as well as some commercial attachés and ambassadors.

Mr Reynolds had just arrived back from Brussels, and he drove from Dublin despite very bad road conditions. He telephoned from Nenagh to say that they had had a bad skid and to go ahead with the meal, but we waited. Mr Cohen had asked for the meeting as he was desperately trying for radome orders and wanted the Irish government to assist. When the meal was over, he summoned us all to a meeting, and we were there until 6 a.m., when we ordered breakfast. Mr Cohen never lost an opportunity to sell. Holding the meeting at the party saved him travelling to Dublin and allowed him to return to America the next day with his family. All the time I was noticing his dedication and persistence, and getting a better understanding of how important it was to have continuous contact with customers. I continued to build up friendships as he directed, and that practice still goes on with new and not-so-new people to this day.

We respected the Americans and their product and formed very close bonds that have lasted our lifetimes and that are now continuing in the next generation. We have known each other now for almost forty-six years. During that time, the steeplejacks, John and I have travelled many miles since we first met our dear friend Carlo Mistretta at Woodcock Hill, and we have made many wonderful memories.

Together we have been to more than eighty different countries selling or carrying out installations. When writing this book, I went through my files to get the names of all the places where we had contracts, and this brought back memories of the times we sent steeplejacks to the Azores, Chitose, Dubai, Denmark, the Faroe Islands, Greenland, Iraq, Iceland, Israel, Jamaica, Libya, Malaysia, Okinawa, Pakistan, Switzerland, Singapore, Spain, the Shetland Islands, Taiwan, Tasmania, Turkey and Zambia. We also worked and travelled throughout the USA, which was amazing – everyone wanted to travel there.

It was a privilege to be able to travel to those countries. Nowadays, Irish people go on holiday to so many exotic places, but back in the 1970s, travelling to do that work was a miracle to us. We felt undeserving so we made sure to get the most out of every opportunity. I felt on occasion that this could not last and that orders would not keep coming, but luckily they did. Only last December, 2015, Collins Steeplejacks had a contract to install a radome in Antarctica.

In the early 1970s, we had several contracts on the Greek mainland and surrounding islands. Before travelling to Greece, I always thought it was a year-round holiday resort with plenty of sun, but when we went up into the mountains our equipment was covered in snow, and there were times when we could not work at all. Though John is a confident driver and accustomed to being on the right-hand side of the road, it was terrifying to drive along a cliff edge and see a sheer drop of hundreds of feet, with no hedge or tree trunk to stop a car going over if anyone made a mistake. It was always a relief to get home to the hotel.

Driving in Athens was an experience because the motorists never stopped blowing their horns. The people were very caring though. We had an agent in Athens, and he and his wife invited us to their home to sample Greek cuisine. They knew which historic sites were worth visiting and took us to see the Acropolis before we left. John had often watched movies about the Greek gods, and he would give me the history of the various monuments, but I did not retain all of it – I just wanted to look and move on.

In the 1970s, we installed a radome in Sofia, Bulgaria. I realised I was not the only female on site when I saw a woman plastering a wall. More women were working on the streets doing what would be considered men's heavy work in Ireland. It was bitterly cold, and I was well padded so no one knew whether I was a man or a woman, and I thought it strange that the women there were wearing skirts.

We worked in the Bahamas and Czechoslovakia and were very often in France. When we worked at Charles de Gaulle and Orly airports, we stayed in five-star hotels and enjoyed fabulous food, but we were often on sites that were very primitive and did not recognise the dishes. We installed a radome at Nantes in western France and stayed in a small hotel with few facilities. It was a civilian site, so I took Susan, who was about eight at the time, and she put the nuts and bolts together. Our English salesman, George Davis, and his wife Dorothy also visited, and they both joined in to help. It was all so casual then. Today that would not be allowed due to health and safety regulations.

We had many contracts in Germany, and, while there, I took the opportunity to go shopping for clothes. I remember being in Frankfurt and seeing a beige and cream reversible coat, skirt, cap and scarf in a shop window. I thought it was a very unusual outfit, so I splashed out. It was fine quality and pricey as were most items there.

We installed the radome at Amsterdam Airport Schiphol and stayed in a city-centre hotel. Amsterdam was a real culture shock. It was beautiful. We toured the canals and cafés at night and popped out to visit the historical sights. We could not go there without taking in a visit to the Rijksmuseum, where we saw the Rembrandts. I bought a copy of his masterpiece, *The Night Watch*, on the street. I had no knowledge of paintings until then, but that gave me an interest. We also went to the Van Gogh Museum and saw the Anne Frank House.

John took a team of steeplejacks to Cerro Potosí in Monterrey, Mexico, to build a radome. The site was almost thirteen thousand feet above sea level. They dined and shopped at Galeana and passed through Saltillo regularly on their way to work. John loved Mexico and loved chatting to the locals. One Mexican told him that President Antonio López de Santa Anna, the nineteenth-century dictator, had formed his army at Saltillo to fight the Texans at the battle of the Alamo.

John was delighted to learn this as he loved American history and had seen the movie about the Alamo starring John Wayne and Richard Widmark.

I had not heard of the Apparitions of Our Lady of Guadalupe at Tepeyac near Mexico City, and they are not well known on this side of the world, but John took steeplejacks near there to do an installation once. He did not usually want to make return visits to countries, but he had no problem when it was America or Mexico. We always went together if contracts came up in that part of the world and had stopovers along the way.

Another interesting trip was to São Paulo, Brazil. We went there to install a radome at the new airport on top of a hundred-foot-high building. We brought our close neighbour, Paul Noonan, to assist. Time pressures did not allow us to see much of the area. Brazil, being a former colony of Portugal, was very different to the rest of South America. We felt privileged to get that contract. When at school, I had learned about São Paulo, but I never envisaged visiting there or even getting to that part of the world.

Paul travelled home, and we flew to Mexico to inspect a radome previously installed at the international airport there. When the work was completed, we went to see the site of the Alamo, in San Antonio. It was eerie to stand on the site where so many had died. When reading the names on the monument, we were surprised to see how many Irish had joined with the Texans to defend the Alamo Mission against the Mexican Army.

We drove past Laredo and El Paso, and it was fascinating to

see signs that we had seen in movies or heard of in songs, like 'The Streets of Laredo' and 'The Cowboy's Lament'. We often went on four-hour mini-tours just to get an idea of the culture of the different cities. We were a bit hindered by the bulky suitcases we carried – they had no wheels back then.

Once, we manoeuvred them to a bus stop in Dallas and a lady sitting at the stop asked if we were visiting and began chatting with us. She was a Scottish lawyer who had an office in downtown Dallas. She told us the tour bus passed her door and offered to mind our luggage while we went to Southfork Ranch to see where the television series *Dallas* was filmed. Later that day we followed the exact same route that President John F. Kennedy took on the day he was shot in 1963.

We could not return home without visiting the Grand Ole Opry in Nashville, Tennessee. Johnny Cash's and Elvis Presley's photographs were everywhere in Nashville, and music blasted from every door. The tour bus passed the homes of many of the stars, including Hank Williams. Their houses were impressive but had so much security that we marvelled at how the rich and famous lived that way. When we were finished, we travelled on for our meetings with Essco in Boston before flying back to Shannon.

Soon after, I went on a trade mission to Russia with the Irish Export Board. We attended an exhibition, gave presentations and met two potential customers. We knew we needed to make a return visit and to keep in regular contact. It was not easy to get around, and you needed to book taxis a day in advance. The security was tight, so knocking on doors was not an option. In the evenings we went to view the Metro or Red

Square, and I felt I had fulfilled a dream. I tried to get tickets for the Bolshoi Ballet but had not realised that it was booked out months in advance.

When John travelled without me, he rarely went on tours. However, one time the customer wanted to use the antenna and the steeplejacks could not work, so they went to Monaco for a few hours to see the Casino Royale and the Riviera. As John put it, it was an experience, and they were a little the poorer afterwards! On another occasion, we had a stopover in San Francisco and crossed over the Golden Gate Bridge. I went to Alcatraz because of the movie *The Birdman of Alcatraz*, which I had seen with John. We also stopped off in Hawaii and visited Pearl Harbor. It was a unique opportunity to see the memorial built in honour of the 1,177 American crewmen who died on the USS *Arizona* on 7 December 1941.

We were awarded a contract in Nairobi, Kenya, at Jomo Kenyatta International Airport. John and I decided we would do this installation ourselves, with another steeplejack, as we knew we would probably never again have the chance to visit that country. Mr Shitaka, the man in charge, was Kenyan but had been educated at Trinity College Dublin. He had married a Dublin girl and they had returned to his homeland. He later became a minister in the Kenyan government. We decided to bring Susan, John and Martina, and were assured by the customer, who later became our friend, that the children would be cared for by his neighbours while we worked. The hotel did not charge for them as they slept in our room. The only extra cost was their food, and we would have had to pay for that regardless of where we were.

Africa had seemed so out of reach, and now here we were visiting, so to me the world had become a smaller place. We had been given a date to be on site, but, when we arrived, the radome had not yet been released from Customs. We had planned to go on a safari after the contract was complete, but when we heard about the delay we decided to go beforehand.

Shortly after setting out for Amboseli National Park, our driver hit a goat. Suddenly men came out from the fields and blocked the road. One man, who was carrying a large knife, and who was naked except for his ornamental necklaces and a piece of leather covering his privates, sat in on the left side of the van beside me. Others surrounded the van. They had knives and all sorts of weapons and were aggressive. We were terrified and wondered what was going to happen. Then tour buses came and stopped to help. We were let go but were stopped again at the end of the tour and the driver had to pay to be allowed to leave. I was concerned that the incident might have affected Martina, who was about three years old. I wondered if this was an omen to turn back.

Later, we went to the Masai Mara National Reserve and were put in shared accommodation with a Peruvian diplomat and his wife. We were lucky to be housed with them as they were getting VIP treatment and we got the same at no extra cost. On the first morning, we were about to leave the cottage to join the tour when the Peruvian lady ran out into the hallway to stop me from going out. She had a tea towel in her hand and opened the door slightly, peeped out and started hitting the ground with the towel. I thought she had gone gaga. We stood behind her to see what was wrong, and there, on the step outside, a huge snake was coiled up – and he was going nowhere! She was a while striking the step before the snake slithered off. Another bad omen. After that, we hung on to the Peruvians' coat-tails. They did not mind: they told us it had been lonely for them on their own and that, being only two people, they always got bad seats. They also told us they loved children – I was glad they liked mine!

We spent the next few days getting up at 5.30 a.m. as that was the best time to see the animals who woke early to hunt for breakfast. One morning, the driver went up close to the animals and parked. Then he opened the roof of the vehicle and told us to keep still and to look to where the lions were waking up. The female stretched, went after the nearest gnu and tore at its back. The unfortunate gnu was roaring and try-ing to escape, then it fell to the ground. The male came with the cubs, and they joined the lioness in eating the gnu while it was still alive. When I booked the safari I had put no thought into what we were going to see. It was a once-in-a-lifetime opportunity, one that could not be missed, but we never forgot that ferocious scene.

Entertainment was provided each day, which was very enjoyable, and different tribes performed traditional dances in very colourful costumes. During one of the shows, I looked down at Martina to see if she was enjoying it, but, to my hor-ror, I saw her forehead was swelling up. She had been stung by something and was having an allergic reaction. The music was very loud, and we were in the middle of a huge crowd. I ran with her to the stage and asked for assistance.

The concert stopped for a moment, and the manager called

for a doctor. We were fortunate that one came to her in minutes and told us to follow him. He packed us all into his jeep and drove very fast for miles over rough terrain, leaving a cloud of dust behind us. Martina's face continued to swell, and she was struggling to breathe. I was frantic, worrying whether or not they would have the necessary facilities where we were going.

We arrived at what appeared to be an army hospital. The doctor acted quickly. He gave Martina an injection and assured us the swelling would soon go down. He was a lovely, caring man, and later he drove us back to see the rest of the concert. Martina was fine after a couple of hours, but I still remember the awful fear to this day.

The next day, the driver and his park warden showed us more animals, driving very close to rhinos and stopping where they were in full view. You would think they would be accustomed to seeing vans and people, but they scraped the ground and looked angry. I told the driver to leave. We did not want to become best friends with this crash of rhinos and were happy to see them in their natural environment from a distance.

The driver tried to start the van but had some trouble with the engine and had to make a couple of attempts to get it going. The guy in the front had a firearm, but what use would it have been if the animals turned the van over or if the engine did not start.

We were absolutely petrified. I asked if we could return to the hotel, but the driver told us there was one more place he wanted to bring us. When we arrived there, he invited us to get out and go to the riverbank to see the hippos in the water. There were many snakes wrapped around trees and on the ground – some too close for comfort. I was happy when we arrived back at our accommodation.

We went for food but encountered monkeys everywhere, even on the tables and chairs. Some were getting too friendly by far and jumped on us while we ate. Apparently it was the norm, but we were frightened when one clung onto Martina and terrified her. The safari was an experience, and very educational, but it was certainly not for me.

We decided not to go out the next day and just stayed at the hotel to swim. We phoned the airport again and were glad to hear that the radome had been released from Customs and would be on site in a couple of days. When it arrived, we completed the installation in record time. The Kenyan people we met were incredible and helped in every way. We forged a lasting friendship with the Shitaka family, and later their son travelled to Ireland and stayed with us in Clonlara for over six months. Our children were younger than he was, but it was a nice experience for them to meet a young man from this very different country.

When Susan finished primary school, we sent her as a boarder to the Salesian Sisters in Brosna, Roscrea. I was very lonely without her. I clearly remember the evening I dropped her off. I had Bambi Cohen and her friend from America with me, and that was a distraction, but I was very sad and cried that night. Susan had just turned twelve. I did feel it was the best thing to do. When John finished primary, we sent him boarding to the Salesian College in Pallaskenry, Co. Limerick.

Our home was very different with the two of them away, and I was broken-hearted. In the beginning, they were only allowed one phone call a week, and we could only see them once a month, but they grew accustomed to the rules and then settled in, and later the rules relaxed and we were able to bring them home at weekends.

The time passed quickly, and it was all worthwhile. Susan and all the girls had their chores, which included getting on their knees to scrub floors. I was delighted that she would know what hard work was all about and felt it was wonderful to learn that kind of discipline. At John's boarding school, they often went to pick potatoes. He loved the outdoors and the work.

When Susan and John finished school, they were very well adjusted. I felt boarding school taught them respect and to be able to take orders. Their education might have been neglected if we had not sent them to boarding school, given our family businesses.

We adopted Hilda, our third daughter and fourth child, when she was four months old and Martina was six. Having a new baby in the house was a beautiful experience, a miracle really. I loved being a mum again, even though I was over forty. Hilda was a real joy. Our whole house changed with her arrival. Josie adored her, as did Mrs Howard, the office staff and the friends and neighbours who came to see her and hold her.

I brought her with me when I took Martina to her Irish dancing lessons, and in no time at all she wanted to go on the floor herself and was hopping around in time to the music. She loved all types of sports and gymnastics and hurled with our local team – they won county medals. When Hilda was six, we discovered she had a real talent for music, and eventually she focused on classical violin. I had always enjoyed traditional music (Co. Clare is well known for Irish music) but never once listened to classical. I developed a real love for the violin just listening to Hilda playing every day. When we had guests, Hilda entertained them and often played jigs and reels while Martina danced.

Buyers often came to the factory to see their radomes being manufactured and tested. We showed them as much of Ireland as we could in the short time they were with us. Some of them came to visit our home and asked about playing golf in the long summer evenings. John took them to the famous Dromoland Castle Golf Club as it was close by. Then he got interested and learned himself. Soon we began playing at Dromoland. Despite a bad start, I managed to hit the ball and enjoyed playing, especially on the short fairways. I always wanted to take my time, but that was not possible on a busy golf course and I was very conscious of holding up other players. We always stood aside and let them pass, but that did disrupt the game.

On the road home one evening, I suggested to John that we build a nine-hole golf course on our farm. The land was centrally located and bordered the river Shannon. It had so much to offer, and the views were very pleasant. I knew there was a niche in the market for a golf course offering cheaper fees that would cater for people like me.

In 1984, I knew of no other person who owned a private golf course in Ireland. Still, I could not see why it would not work. We had little money and interest rates were around 18 per cent, but for some reason that did not deter us. We had some knowledge of what was required, we had enthusiasm, and we had a passion to succeed. We could do the work over a long period of time as we accumulated money, and I anticipated getting a grant.

I had a vision that one day we could add a leisure centre. The river Shannon was a real asset and could be used for swimming, walks and boating, and a tennis court and games room could be added when the time was right. I visualised getting golfers from Clonlara and the surrounding villages, from Limerick City, Ennis and Shannon. We knew we could go after golf outings for the core business. Without much planning, we went ahead. We did not have enough land to extend if the venture was successful, so I approached local farmers and found some who were willing to sell and one who we could depend on for more land if needed and at a reasonable price.

I put the options in place and then took on the challenge of building a golf course. We asked the local community in Clonlara for their views and told them our vision for the project. They encouraged us in every way and promised their full support. We met with Noel Cassidy, who was the professional at Castletroy Golf Club and a Limerick man. He was very positive and worked with John on designing the course. He was very generous with his time.

I had no idea of the enormity of the project we were undertaking, which was just as well. I knew we would be working with soil, and I was well acquainted with that, having come from a farm. It was not hi-tech, but we would require a golf expert to guide us, hard-working staff, money and dedication. The physical work began, and the fairways, tee boxes and greens soon took shape. We knew it would take time to improve them and to bring them up to standard.

Duncan Gray (a Scotsman) stands out in my mind as being beyond generous to us. Duncan was the golf-course manager in Lahinch, Co. Clare, and, though he had returned to Scotland, he said that he would be back and forth and would continue to call and give advice. On one of his visits, the conversation turned to touring motor homes. I told him that I was fascinated with them – we had hired one once and were considering buying a small one, although I worried that I would not be able to drive it or manage all those gadgets if John were not about. We went back to talking about the golf course, and I thought no more about it. A week later, I received a call from Duncan saying that he had picked up a second-hand motor home and that his wife was on her way to Clonlara from Scotland with it. Several hours later, she drove into our driveway with our new home on wheels. We gave her a real Irish welcome. We refunded the money, but we never forgot that kindness, and that little motor home was put to excellent use.

Duncan kept his promise and called to meet John, Mike and Eddie, who worked on the course under his guidance. The most difficult part was getting the greens right. The man-made lakes and sand bunkers were coming along, and we were delighted with the results. Other areas had to be drained into the Shannon. A stream ran across the land and the bridges acted as features. The planted trees divided the fairways and, in time, we saw a golf course emerge.

I walked the course very early each morning to look for protruding roots, stones or any objects that might damage the mowers and would leave a mark so the man cutting the fairways would see them. It was my exercise for the day. I brought a Dictaphone with me to make notes of any money-making ideas that came to mind that would finance the project. I longed for the day when golfers would be able to play and money would come in.

We were told that if we joined the Golfing Union of Ireland and followed its rules and standards, we would have to apply for a licence and eventually have a clubhouse, but it was not an immediate requirement so we put that out of our heads. Then the Angler's Rest pub next door came up for sale. It was a well-known historical building facing the famous Falls of Doonass and the local graveyard. We had been there many times, attending funerals and praying at the Holy Well nearby, and we rarely missed the annual pilgrimage on 15 August. The pub had a car park and accommodation and was right on the bank of the river where children could paddle and adults could enjoy a swim. It was magical during the summer months when barbecues and Irish dancing were going on and the music could be heard right up the river.

It was an ideal opportunity to get a licence, and so we bought it. We got it up and running very quickly, and money began to come in. We were very popular with visitors and with locals who came for the salmon fishing. However, I had absolutely no experience of the bar business and I had no systems in place. We continued on regardless; somehow I felt we must be making money as we were able to pay for stock and seemed to have a satisfactory margin, but that did not mean we were making a profit. It was a cash business, very labour-intensive, and it took a long time to collect the small amounts from so many different areas. However, the crowds kept coming and the atmosphere was brilliant.

At the same time, we were trying to improve the facilities around the golf course. We converted some of the old outhouses to changing rooms and put in showers and lockers. Another outhouse was turned into a games room with a pool table, gaming machines and table tennis. Later, we put in an outdoor tennis court near the original orchard. The gate lodge and other outhouses became guest accommodation, which was very popular and brought in badly needed income. We were Bord Fáilte-approved, and they came regularly to inspect this leisure centre, so we had to keep up standards.

I continued to bring paperwork home at night. I wanted to know how the tourist industry worked but had no time to understand the stocktaking and the bar trade. I considered adding an extension to the Angler's Rest to allow for larger functions. We built the walls and had it roofed but realised that it was all growing too big to be just a side business, with Collins Steeplejacks and Essco Collins as well as my Irish and international travel commitments, so we did not finish the interior.

The business continued to flourish beyond our expectations. I put in a manager to run the pub and to meet budgets, but it did not work out. The operation was too big for one person to cover seven days and too small to justify hiring two people. Either we would have to be able to have weddings, conferences and other functions, or we would have to cut back, and that would be difficult to do. It would mean closing some parts, like the dance hall, or only opening in the evenings, and I felt that would confuse customers.

Everyone involved was doing their best, but no one knew the exact financial situation. Seeing so many people and so much cash did not necessarily mean profit, and that was a real worry to me. I continued on working in the dark, but in the back of my mind I knew action had to be taken.

I never turned down the opportunity to give a talk when invited, as I always wanted to promote our business. Giving and attending talks kept our name out there and sometimes brought work through the contacts I made. At one event at the Irish Management Institute in Dublin, in around 1985, I met Mr Feargal Quinn, businessman and television personality, for the first time, and met Margaret Heckler again. I also met Victor Kiam, the President of Remington, who had written a book about his life as an entrepreneur.

During the Q&A session, a businessman said, 'I have always admired you, Angela, but now I think you are making a mistake going into the tourist business. It is so different to what you do.' I didn't agree with him, of course, but I did not say that at the time. He himself was in the steel business and soon after went into the tourist business, just as I had done. I imagine we both learned a lot. But I always remember that comment, and it was true: the tourist business did not suit me.

7

Cork Great Race

One morning, I was on my way to work when I developed a terrible sharp pain in my side. I continued on to my office, and Margaret Leland, my secretary, drove me to the doctor. It turned out that I had a large cyst on my ovary. I went to Limerick Regional Hospital to have it removed. Thankfully, it was benign. Afterwards, the surgeon told me he had not been able to save my ovary but assured me the remaining ovary would do the work of two.

The twelve days in hospital and my subsequent recovery caused me to fall behind in my work, and there was a bit of chaos. John was far away on a radome contract, but our employees were brilliant. We had two Margarets and Noreen Slattery at the time, as well as some part-timers, trying to cope and take bookings for the leisure centre on top of doing their own work in Collins Steeplejacks. We were laying out aerial materials for the men up to 2 a.m. and were then back in the office again for 8 a.m. Noreen would be at home working on the invoices through the night, while Josie took charge of the house and the four children and fed everyone who called.

Despite so much going on and the pressure, we had lively

craic and no one complained. It sounds strange to say that it was very exciting having to meet deadlines. We laughed together and produced results at the same time. But it was a real shock to realise that something so serious could happen so suddenly.

In 1985, Cork was celebrating the eight-hundredth anniversary of its first charter from Prince John in 1185. I was asked to be involved in a 'Great Race' with well-known personalities such as David Boyce, Eddie English, Mike Murphy, Gerry Kiernan, Demi Fitzgerald, Tim McGrath, Finbarr Warren and Ray Cummins, all undertaking different challenges for charity. Mine was to climb the County Hall in Cork City.

It was agreed that I would do a practice climb, so Denis Horgan (the organiser) would know what was involved. The plan was that I would hang on the jib of the crane and the driver would swing me onto the ladders on the County Hall. A few days before, I was out in the sun without protection and got badly sunburnt. I had to proceed – a crane had already been hired and people were organised to be at the County Hall, so I kept applying cream and taking painkillers while John drove to Cork from Clonlara.

As we reached Cork City, I decided I had to see a doctor as I was in awful pain. John saw a brass nameplate on a wall off Wilton Road and pulled in. As I approached the sign, I saw it was for a veterinary clinic and went back to tell him. He said, 'Go back in anyway, he might do something for you!' We still laugh about this when I remind him that he took me to the vet!

We had no more time to waste locating a doctor, so we

continued on and I did the trial climb. I will never forget the pain of that sunburn, and ever since I try to stay out of the sun.

On the day of the Great Race, 16 June 1985, huge crowds assembled, including our families and staff. I got onto the jib of the crane, and the driver swung me up and around to let the crowds see, then he moved the jib nearer to the seventeen-storey County Hall. At two hundred and nineteen feet, it was the tallest building in the State.

I manoeuvred myself off the jib in mid-air (at about one hundred and fifty feet) and onto the ladders. I know this was mad. I see that now. I depended totally on the driver not to move while I transferred from his crane to the ladders. That part went perfectly well, but I was trembling because I was not accustomed to climbing in the presence of large crowds and cameras. Then the crane was taken away. I climbed from there to the top, a distance of about seventy feet.

When I reached the top, I stood on the ledge, over two hundred feet from the ground, and turned around to wave. Later, Martina, who was only eight, told me that frightened her. Up to then, and to my regret, I never thought of my children when I was doing these things. I should have thought of how they would feel, but it never occurred to me until that comment.

Pat Cox, the RTÉ reporter, was on the rooftop with his camera crew. (Pat, a Limerick man, went on to be a politician and later became President of the European Parliament.) He was very friendly. He knew I was nervous and for a couple of minutes he did all the talking, then asked many questions, which helped me greatly. After that, there was a break for the

RTÉ crew to meet the other competitors, and then I was to climb down.

For the descent, I had decided it would be more exciting for the crowd to see me hanging on a chair-line, lowering myself from the top, instead of climbing down the vertical ladders again. However, I underestimated the recesses on the façade of the County Hall. Climbing down the outside of a building with a smooth surface is really easy, but the glass recessed façade of the County Hall, with its concrete pillars, is far from smooth. On my trial climb I aimed for the pillars and was fine, but this time I was not always able to aim for them as I was not concentrating and was nervous with the cameras and crowds below.

Once I missed the first pillar, I panicked. I went inwards towards the windows, then spun back out. The rope twirled, and I struck my head. This continued because I had no control, and, having never experienced that before, I did not know what to do. I could not reconnect the microphone to tell John and the steeplejacks on top, so I did the only thing I could, which was to wave and smile and pretend this was all part of the entertainment. But it was not really a smile, it was a grimace of pain.

The bumping hurt and I knew I could not bear much more of it. I wondered if John and the men above knew that the descent was not going according to plan. When I was about three-quarters of the way down, still bumping around, John looked over the top, saw me spinning and realised my predicament. Immediately he fed me more rope, which allowed me to drop quickly to the ground. The skin on the palms of my hands was peeled off and burnt in places – which had not been in the plan either.

When it comes to competition, I throw caution to the wind, and it was worth it on that occasion. I would do it again if I had to. It was a wonderful, exciting day. At the celebratory dinner that evening, Mr Peter Malone, Manager of Jury's Hotel, announced that I was the winner of the Great Race. I had not done anything great or unusual, but it was lovely to win just the same. I received a silver plaque mounted on a wooden frame, which I still have. John, a staunch Corkman (and he never lets me forget it), is especially proud of it. The judges for the race were Clayton Love, Chairman of Beamish & Crawford; Lucette Murray, Director of Cork 800; Captain Michael Dalton of Aer Lingus; Martin Dully, Chief Executive of Aer Rianta; and Captain Frank Laycock, Director of Irish Helicopters Ltd. The race coordinator of the day was Captain Ron Sivewright, Chief Training Officer of Irish Helicopters.

Some will remember 1986 as the year Jack Charlton arrived in Ireland, while others will recall it as the year Knock Airport was opened, having been built by the local parish priest, Monsignor Horan, with help from his community and the Irish government. We remember it for many reasons – the saddest being the death, on 7 September, of John's mother, Nora O'Mahony. We received a phone call to say she had died suddenly, just a short time after her heart bypass operation. She had been complaining for a couple of days, but her death was totally unexpected.

We all loved her, especially her grandchildren. She was the glue that held us all together. When she died, the house lost its heart, and her family were devastated. Mrs O'Mahony was a beautiful person, always kind and fair. She worked outside and inside the house, and when she sat down she did her knitting and often played cards. She took care of the family – and the farm, when John's dad was working with us. She was the eldest of a family of five children. When she was just thirteen, and her youngest sibling only a few years old, their mother died, on Christmas Day. Nora had to take responsibility for her siblings while dealing with her own grief.

We often went shopping to Limerick, and I remember she paid £7 for my wedding going-away outfit – that treat was special to me. She had also paid for my engagement ring. I loved her and pray to her to this day. Mrs O'Mahony was buried in the new cemetery in Millstreet, Co. Cork.

I often think of how life goes on, no matter what happens. Three weeks after Mrs O'Mahony's funeral, we had the golf course to open. Though not completely ready, we needed the income, and so, with the Angler's Rest and the amenities already up and running, we planned the official opening for 27 September 1986. To ensure the day went well, we sought the help of a golf expert, Mr Myles Murphy, who arranged sponsorship, organised teams and invited the famous Mr Christy O'Connor to be the guest of honour.

We decided that all the money from the day – from the golfers, the bar, the dancing, the face-painting, stalls, pony rides and the masterclass by Christy O'Connor – would be divided evenly between the Limerick and Clare Youth Centres. Sr Joan Bowles was head of the Limerick Youth Centre, and Fr Sean Sexton head of Clare. One night, they were both sitting in our kitchen with John and me, writing out a list of the events to be held. We did not notice the time was 1.30 a.m., and we wanted an idea for an article we were preparing. Without thinking, we made a call to Eugene Phelan, Editor of the *Limerick Leader*, waking him up. He amazed me: he was so gracious and answered our questions as if it were midday. That was just one example of the help we received.

Susan was eighteen years old and John was fifteen at the time. Susan had already spent a year in University College Cork (UCC), but she took the next year out to assist with the launch of the golf and leisure centre. She and John put forward their idea of having a weekend carnival to get the young people to attend. The *Clare Champion, Limerick Leader, Cork Examiner, Tipperary Star* and the local radio stations in Clare and Limerick gave us lots of coverage, so people came from far and near. We enjoyed fine weather, and a great day was had by all. The event raised £10,000, and we were delighted that it was such a success. It ended with a prize-giving at the Angler's Rest. That memory is still with those who attended, and we still chat about it.

I missed the prize-giving as I had to leave early on the Sunday to travel to the UK with Martina for an important dancing competition. I used the trip to meet travel agents and to deliver brochures for the new business. We went to Wembley Stadium to hand out leaflets to people coming out from a match. Martina, who was nine years old, gave them out at one side of the entrance while I was at the other. Standing at the gate with our suitcases, handing out leaflets, was a bit embarrassing, and I had to push myself to do it. I felt sorry for

Martina but knew that training was necessary and you do what you have to do.

As a result of our work, some travel agents visited to see what we were offering, and many English visitors came, especially children on school trips, as we offered reasonable dormitory accommodation. And Martina got to dance in her competition as well, so the trip was a real success.

John and I were in a bad place after his mother's death. We were learning a new business and keeping pace with Collins Steeplejacks and Essco Collins. I knew I could not keep up, and I often felt our bubble would burst – and it almost did. One morning in early 1987, we were all doing our own work when someone looked at the diary to see what was on for the day. We had a golf outing from Galway, and caterers had been hired to provide food. John then told us that he was having his local golf-club outing on that day too. We could only cater for one large group. We had a mini crisis on our hands with the double booking and I knew I had to make a decision.

I decided to go with the group from Galway as their booking was in the diary and there would be a loss of income if we didn't. I made my decision based on fairness and emphasised to all that it was crucial to note bookings if things were to run smoothly. John's outing had not been noted in the diary, and, because it was local, we could contact everyone and explain what had happened. Most were known to us and to the staff, and they would understand it had been a human error. When contacted, they were very understanding that these things happen, and we made it up to them afterwards. Our local golfers were very important to us.

John was very angry at my decision, and it was our first and only serious row. He would never argue – he would just go silent and leave me talking to myself – but on this occasion he moved out of our bedroom for the first time in the twenty years we had been married. We were part of a small family business that worked closely together, but, despite that, the disagreement became very public and was well known in our offices, within both families and beyond. We both worked together, so it was awkward for staff. I wrote him notes and they delivered them and brought back his reply. We had picture but no sound! At the time it was very serious, but now, looking back, we seem so childish. However, our pride prevailed and neither one wanted to give in. I can see how situations evolve as a result of stubbornness.

I wonder what would have happened if I had not received that nice phone call telling us we were to be given the Bowmaker Award for Irish Industry, which ended our sulking and silence – much to the relief of everyone. The call was from Mr Peter Colgan of Bowmaker Bank, and he told me that the presentation would be made by John Bruton, Minister of Finance, at a luncheon in Dublin.

Three hundred people attended on the day – all types of dignitaries: people from government departments, ambassadors, foreign visitors, our American and Irish business colleagues and our own family and friends. It was a very pleasant occasion, and the only pressure was making a speech to such a distinguished group. I had a script, which I did not stick to as I was so nervous. I shortened it and it was fine. We received a solid bronze sculpture of Queen Maeve of Connaught and £5,000, which we gave to our employees.

Nuala Ní Dhomhnaill had her Irish television programme *Súil Thart* at the time, and she came to film our golf and leisure centre. That was a unique opportunity to promote our business. Nuala, a fluent Irish-speaker, interviewed many Irish-speakers, including teachers from Clonlara and the surrounding areas. Her crew filmed tennis players enjoying their game, people riding horses and using the sports facilities and anglers fishing on the bank of the river.

The whole community rallied around to assist on the day, and traditional musicians and storytellers provided music and entertainment. We were a group networking together to promote the amenities available to tourists in the region. Martina, who had just won the Irish Dancing World Championship, was invited to perform, and she and her friends made their teachers proud. Christy O'Connor came to play a few holes of golf and was filmed on our course chatting to Nuala. It was fantastic exposure and helped put the golf course on the map. We greatly appreciated that assistance.

Soon after, I developed another severe pain and went to the doctor. He found another lump and sent me to hospital. The surgeon removed it, but it was so large he could not save my remaining ovary. Being in hospital and recovering afterwards was difficult. I could not afford to be out of work, so I returned. I was catching up but not feeling great, so I went back to the doctor. He sent me back to have more examinations, and I had to have a hysterectomy and appendectomy. This meant ten more days in hospital and weeks to recover.

The doctor gave me the bad news that the menopause would come right away. I was about forty-three years old. Life was never the same again. The hot flushes were the worst, as I could not sleep, and not getting enough rest was devastating. I was advised to take things easy, but that was difficult with two-year-old Hilda, and Martina, who was about nine. Blushing at business meetings was embarrassing. I was losing the confidence that I had gained.

The golf and leisure centre and our amenities were being talked about a great deal, and I received our first significant inquiry about holding a conference. It was from a group of young Limerick executives who were trying to put business our way. The plan was that the people attending would stay at the self-catering cottages and dormitories and in the B&B at the Angler's Rest. I had several meetings with the organisers, and everything was agreed.

All that remained was that they come and pay the deposit, and that meeting was arranged to take place at the Angler's Rest. However, because we had temporary staff coming and going, I was not made aware of it.

When the night of the meeting arrived, John was in France, and I was in bed recovering from my operation when Susan came running up to tell me there were lots of people standing outside the door in the dark. When I did not turn up at the Angler's Rest, they had walked up through the golf course to the house.

I went downstairs to explain, but we lost our conference and had the embarrassment of it all. I did not try to defend our actions or to pursue the business, as it would have been inappropriate. I hoped there would be other opportunities. There was nothing to say except that we had not been told about the meeting and I had just come out of hospital, but that was not their problem.

The barman working on that bleak wintry Monday night was unaware of their visit, so the group did not even get a cup of tea or a drink. They were very understanding but were disappointed. When I meet those people around now, they tell me they have long forgotten about it, but I can still feel the shame and embarrassment of letting them down. It was another serious indication that it was time to examine our situation. We valued our name, and now we had cancelled a golf outing and had lost a conference, which could have been the first of many.

One day, in March 1988, John and I were just setting out from Clare to Coleraine, Co. Londonderry, Northern Ireland, when we received a telephone call to say that Mrs Howard was dying. She had been in hospital for a couple of weeks but had seemed fine when we visited.

We were fortunate to arrive in time. She knew that we were all there, and, after an hour or so, she passed away. It meant a great deal to me that we were present. It was very sad, especially for John as it was his seventeenth birthday and she had minded him when he was a baby. They had always been very close. She had always been there to pick him up when he fell, and I had not, like most mothers when they drop their children to the crèche.

Not a day went by without her saying, 'Be happy let ye' and 'God guard ye and mind ye.' She had no children and took care of ours as if they were her own. She gave a big welcome to everyone who called, including the steeplejacks – she knew them all. On the day of her funeral, they carried her coffin, and she got a great send-off. I still have her missal and little prayers, which I use regularly.

I was discovering that the tourist industry was not for me and that the centre needed experts to run and develop it. Improvements had to be made before something more serious happened. I considered taking on a partner or selling the business. We struggled with the idea and finally decided that selling was our only option. The centre was at its peak, with tourists, adult groups on courses, cyclists, golfers and school groups from all over Europe and as far away as Japan coming to visit. It was the right time to sell. It was hard to call a halt right when the whole place was booming, but after the operations and being out of work for so long, I was struggling and very unwell. Selling was the correct option.

In September 1989, we contacted an auctioneer to put our property up for sale. We had made a huge effort to put everything in order and have the grounds and chalets looking pretty. Deep down, I knew I would settle for less than the asking price, as I was not sorry to be parting with the golf course and leisure centre, or the Angler's Rest, but we knew we would get near the asking price.

There was a demand for a course for the middle-of-the-road golfer. We had a new and unusual product, bordered by the river Shannon and with great views. The location was wonderful, right between Shannon and Limerick and so many surrounding villages.

Most of the national newspapers carried the story, which was very beneficial. What was intriguing to us was that some very important people came to view the property – some even landed on the lawn in their helicopters. There were some dodgy viewers also. Most were offering near our asking price, but we wanted to wait a while in case there was enough interest to spark a bidding war.

Then, one Friday, the auctioneer called us to say he had a party from the UK who were very interested and who would pay full price. He came over with Michael and Jill O'Connell, who were in Ireland for the weekend purely to buy a property. We had a great feeling about them and knew they were serious buyers. They viewed the house and walked the course and saw that the place was alive and buzzing. They made an offer on the same day.

It was lower than the asking price, but we knew that it was their first offer. We began negotiating, and there was a series of calls that went on for several hours. Then the calls stopped, and we thought nothing more would happen before Monday. We assumed they were off looking at other properties over the Saturday and Sunday.

We were having our normal Sunday at home when, to our absolute surprise and astonishment, Mr and Mrs O'Connell arrived at our door. It would have been easier to negotiate over the telephone, and I would have been braver, but there they were. Whoosh! They came straight to the point and told me that they wanted the property and had come to make a final offer. They wanted to return to England that evening with the deal struck.

I was petrified that we would say something that might jeopardise the sale. We were talking big money, which we had never dreamed of getting, and I had not dealt with amounts that large before. I did not want to get my zeros mixed up, and, with the auctioneer not being there, we were nervous.

Mrs O'Connell looked around the house again, then walked out to the golf course, leaving her husband in the kitchen with us to strike a deal, but we talked so much that when she came back no negotiating had been done. She was only back a few minutes when she asked if we had reached an agreement. I was dumbfounded. She then asked if we could get back to talking business, and there and then she put an offer to us.

We were totally thrown because it was close to our asking price, but I felt we should ask for more. I found a notepad and pen to give me time to prepare myself and began writing. My palms were perspiring and my heart was thumping so loudly I thought they could hear it. I remembered back to when I attended the fairs in Tulla with my father, over forty years before, and heard him bargaining. The buyers and sellers would hold tough for ages. All that knowledge stood to me that day.

The buyers increased their offer. We refused it (as you do) and haggled again until we finally agreed on a figure. It was all done in the space of an hour. Mrs O'Connell was a shrewd businesswoman. When the figure was agreed, we shook hands on it, just as they did in the old days, except we didn't spit on our palms. We then had tea, and they headed back to England. Delight, satisfaction and worry all went through our minds: we could not believe what we had just done. The joy of getting a buyer was overwhelming.

We called the auctioneer the following morning and gave him the news that the leisure centre had been sold and sent in a list of what had been agreed. It helped that he was a great friend, who had been in the Gardaí with John before he started his own business. He was happy for us and it was no hassle to him.

Once the deposit was paid, we had to act quickly because the new buyers wanted to move in within a couple of months. They told us they would be applying for a club licence (which they did and were successful), so they did not buy the Angler's Rest. We advertised and sold that separately.

I dreamed of moving to a quiet area and looked forward to never hearing a doorbell ring again. When we started out in Clonlara, we just wanted to live in an old country house, but when we developed the leisure centre, that changed everything. We lived in the main house right in the middle of all the action and had no privacy. There was noise seven days a week, around the clock. Many people arrived in the middle of the night, having come by boat to Dublin or Rosslare and driven straight to us. It was a very successful business venture and made a profit, and we were very happy that we had built it. But it took its toll. Things might have been different if we had a home away from the centre. I could not describe the feeling when it became somebody else's responsibility. I still say that the tourist industry is a tough business and that money made from it is hard earned.

We found a property in Ardnacrusha, not far from Clonlara and only four miles on the Clare side of Limerick City. We were fortunate to have money from the sale to pay all our bills, to buy a home and to have some left over to invest. Prior to the sale, we had no savings or pension, and money meant nothing to John and me. Now we were in a very different position.

The packing was traumatic as we had accumulated tons of stuff over the years, but it was exciting to be going to a new address. The new property was a well-designed stud farm – too large and not what we wanted, but there wasn't anything else available at the time. We moved in but asked the auctioneer to keep it up for sale. If he found a buyer, we would move again. We had little use for seventeen stables, thirty-eight acres of land, sheds and outbuildings. (We were still living there over twenty-five years later.)

I arrived in Ardnacrusha a complete wreck. I had dreamed about new furnishings and had looked forward to all the DIY, sewing, designing and matching fabrics, but this time the spark wasn't there, and I found it hard to settle in and get familiar with our new surroundings. I was feeling my age but tried to be positive and convince myself I was only in my prime. I blamed the sudden onset of the menopause for many of my problems.

As the months passed, I had to make a real effort to go to work. I had thought leaving the tourist industry and moving to a quiet area would make a major change, but it was not happening.

Susan went to Australia for a year. I decided to visit her there and to combine it with a business trip. It would be my last extensive one due to health and our change in direction. We went out from Shannon and spent time in America on the way, then we went to meet her in Sydney. The pace of life in Sydney was slow and people had time to chat. It was similar to Ireland back in the 1950s. Australia is a marvellous country, so friendly and like Ireland in some ways, but it is too far from home – I could not live there. I think John would though.

I had an interesting experience looking from the apartment towards the Opera House and the Sydney Harbour Bridge. A plane and a helicopter were in the sky above the bridge and underneath were a water taxi and a cruiser, side by side, while buses, cars and a train were crossing over. It was the first time I had seen so many modes of transport together and it was a very different image from my home in Kilkishen. I always drew comparisons between where I came from and where I found myself at any given time. I knew I was very lucky.

I was not lonely leaving Susan as I knew she would soon be coming back. We stopped over in New Zealand and found the people very similar to those in Australia. Then we went to Beijing via Hong Kong to meet with Mr Zhou Yang, the former Chinese Ambassador to Ireland, and his wife and family. We had remained friends and had been corresponding with each other. I thought now that he was back in China he might help procure another order for Essco.

Mr Zhou picked me up at Beijing Airport, and we had several meetings, but nothing came of them. We stood in Tiananmen Square and saw the Gate of Heavenly Peace, but, despite its size, beauty and history, my only thought was of the 1989 student protests and the massacre that followed when military tanks rolled over them and innocent civilians. The image has not faded with time. But I was glad to have seen Tiananmen Square, and the Great Wall.

After a week with Mr Zhou, we returned to Ireland via Hong Kong and London. Despite our many visits, including that one, and our close friendship, we received no more orders from China. Many years later, we discovered that the Chinese had copied our product and had begun to produce a Chinese version.

I was invited by the National Council for Educational Awards (NCEA) and the Higher Education and Training Awards Council (now Quality and Qualifications Ireland, the governing body that awards degrees to PhD level to all third-level colleges outside of universities) to attend meetings in Dublin. They were inviting heads of industry to meet with the various colleges and discuss with lecturers what job skills were required by employers, and they were anxious to have input from a woman in business.

I was very flattered to be invited and knew it would raise the profile of our companies. I was not feeling well at the time but volunteered regardless. I soon found that I could not give the work the attention it required. I was the only female, and should have done my bit for women, but I just was not able. I gave notice but promised I would go back when I was better. It was very necessary and interesting work.

Due to the upsurge of industrial expansion in Ireland there were many job opportunities, especially for technicians. Colleges did not want to be disconnected and were making sure they had courses that would equip candidates with the skills to meet the needs of employers. I was especially interested in courses that would encourage women to think outside the box and go for positions other than teaching, nursing and the civil service, which were often difficult to get. The team and I were looking at these issues and engaging with many companies.

During the first week in August 1992, when I was still with

Susan in Australia, I had received a telephone call to say that I was to be conferred with an honorary doctorate by the NCEA for my contribution to my community. I did not know what that meant except that it was a great honour and that I felt undeserving.

When the day arrived, 30 November 1992, John drove us all to Dublin Castle where the ceremony was to take place. On arrival, I was taken upstairs to a dressing room, while John, Susan, John, Martina and Hilda went in to a great hall to take their seats.

I saw the then Taoiseach, Albert Reynolds, whom I admired greatly and whom I knew through our business with Essco. He came to our annual dinner dances. We were fitted with our robes and told where to wait. I talked and paced around and pretended like I did this every day. Then we headed in a procession down the ornate winding stairs to the hall. We followed members of the NCEA, professors and invited guests – all in robes. I saw my family in the second row as I walked by. I gave them a smile, and we went on and were seated in the front.

Two others were conferred before me so when my turn came I knew what to do. I walked up with Mr Gerry Lee, Director of Buildings and Development, University College Galway, and stood in front of the Taoiseach and the other dignitaries at the head table. When Mr Lee read from the lectern, I thought he was speaking about someone else, not me. I always find it difficult to take a compliment – as do most people.

When he was finished, he said, 'Chairman, I am pleased to present Mrs Angela Collins O'Mahony to the Council for admission to the degree Doctor of Laws honoris causa, and

I ask you, Chairman, to confer that degree.' I walked up the steps and Mr Tom Cullivan put on my cap and showed me where to sign the register. Then the Chairman of the NCEA, Richard Healy, asked Albert Reynolds to present the parchment. Photographs were taken, after which I went back to my seat and waited until the ceremony was complete, very humbled by the whole event.

Later, we stood on the stairs leading from the great hall for more photographs. I was placed beside the Taoiseach and the seven other newly conferred honorary doctors: Mr Hywel Ceri Jones, Director of the EC Task Force for Human Resources, Education Training and Youth; Pádraig Mac Diarmada, Director and Co-founder of the NCEA; Patrick Donegan, a prominent trade unionist and educationalist; Gay Corr, the Principal of Galway Regional Technical College; Pádraig Faulkner, former Minister for Education; Kevin Killeen, former CEO of Waterford Vocational Education Committee; and John Charles Nagle, former Secretary of the Department of Agriculture.

The next day, I was bowled over when I was told to buy the *Irish Independent* as it had a photo of Hilda and me on its front page. *The Irish Times*, *The Cork Examiner*, *Clare Champion* and *Limerick Leader* carried the story, as did several magazines. We were fortunate and grateful to get such coverage. As an honorary doctor, I was invited to subsequent ceremonies, including the conferring of an honorary doctorate on Patrick Hillery, the former President of Ireland (and a Clareman), and Baroness Nuala O'Loan, the first Police Ombudsman of Northern Ireland. She was so down to earth. I sometimes look at those holding very important positions and think they are very different to me, but when we meet I wonder why I had that perception of them in the first place.

We met Jean Kennedy Smith when she was being conferred. She is a sister of John F. Kennedy and was American Ambassador to Ireland during the Bill Clinton presidency. It was lovely to be able to meet such a famous person and tell her about our association with the Essco radome company in Boston. We told her how our joint venture had come about and how Essco came to Ireland and joined with Collins Steeplejacks. She was interested in the story, especially as it involved Boston, which was very dear to her.

It was the same with Dr Joyce O'Connor and Judge Catherine McGuinness, conferred in April 2008, and Seamus Mallon, who was involved in the Peace Talks. He endeared himself to us right away. We also met my friend, television celebrity and businessman, Feargal Quinn. They were all previous recipients of honorary doctorates.

Mr Cohen called often, and during one of his calls he suddenly mentioned finding a buyer for his companies. I knew he had many health issues and that his daughters were not interested in his radome factories, but for some reason I thought that he would continue on, or even keep the factory in Kilkishen. I never imagined he would retire.

It came as a shock. For us, the joint venture with Essco had been very worthwhile and made it possible for us to build a golf course with the dividends and the sale of our shares. I thought of my own situation and retirement sounded nice. I look back now and see how the actions of others affect us. We were a bit like sheep, I suppose. From that moment, the word 'retiring' took hold. We had invested our money wisely, and it was bringing an extra income, so we were comfortable.

I actively discouraged Susan and John from going into the steeplejack business because many factories were closing, spires were no longer being built and some were being lowered instead. New building practices and new methods were being introduced, and it was difficult getting certified steeplejacks. I wanted our children to have careers and to get secure govern-ment employment. I see now that I was so tired I was passing on my negativity to them instead of letting them follow their dreams. I did not realise that the steeplejack business was all they wanted.

I knew that Susan and John had enjoyed working in the office, answering the phone, bookkeeping, adding columns and running errands. John had gone out on sites with his father and with the steeplejacks and had loved it. They had heard us talking about the steeplejacks and radomes from morning to night and wanted that same buzz.

I had insisted that they go to college. Susan was sixteen years old when she sat the Leaving Certificate, and she went straight to UCC, staying in a flat in Cork and returning home at weekends. She achieved her BA and HDip and later became a secondary-school teacher. After her year in Australia, she taught in Kilmallock, Co. Limerick; Rockwell College, Co. Tipperary; and Castlebar, Co. Mayo.

John had experience meeting tourists at Clonlara when we had the golf course, and, after completing his Leaving Certificate, he studied Hotel Management at the Athlone

Institute of Technology, spending three years there. During that time, he got work experience at Dromoland Castle Hotel, Newmarket-on-Fergus, Co. Clare. He went on work experience to Switzerland and, later, to Jury's Hotel in Limerick. On completion, he was offered a position at Kilternan Golf and Country Club, but he liked being near home and took a permanent position at the Ardhú Ryan Hotel in Limerick as Restaurant Manager. John loved people, was respectful and was a great worker. While he seemed happy, he always wanted to be his own boss. He too was planning to do what he loved: to be in the steeplejack business.

I was not worried about Martina, as she was only thirteen and in secondary school at the Laurel Hill Coláiste, which was an excellent all-Irish school in Limerick. Hilda was only six and in primary school at Saint Philomena's in Limerick. I was glad to have the opportunity now to spend more time with them and was partly fulfilling my dream of life as a stay-at-home mother.

Martina had been learning Irish dancing since the age of seven, and she began to win championships at about nine. Because of that, we travelled a great deal. She had her first win at the All Scotland Championships and later won the Great Britain Championship. She was a World Champion a couple of times in the late 1980s. I entered her in the North American Irish Dance Championships, and she had success in both Chicago and New York. She gave up Irish dancing in 1992, when she was fourteen, to study for the Junior Certificate.

When *Riverdance* came on television in April 1994, I worried that she might not go on to do her Leaving Certificate.

The money was tempting, and many of her friends joined and toured. I did not have to worry as she had her heart set on becoming a solicitor and worked hard to get the points to go to University College Dublin (UCD). She was there for three years and received her law degree. She became a solicitor in 2002.

Hilda came with us when I took Martina to dancing, and she learned to dance herself when she was about four. She loved it. Then a teacher came to her primary school to give violin lessons, and she became interested in that. We drove her to the *feiseanna* (Irish music competitions), and she was always placed first or second. Music took more time than dancing as Hilda had to go to theory lessons as well as music lessons, and she had to be taken to an accompanist and attend orchestras, recitals and concerts. She spent hours with her violin. It was very demanding on top of her homework; however, it was all worthwhile. I loved my new life.

8

Beating Colon Cancer

Five days after our celebrations in Dublin Castle for my honorary doctorate, on the morning of 5 December 1992, I received the sad call to say that my mother had died during the night. We had visited her regularly, and my brother Paddy and his wife Mary were with her the previous evening, but there had been no sign that death was imminent.

Mam was eighty-seven, a great age, and many would say it was a relief to her. However, all of us who have lost a mother know that when you hear the words 'she passed away', irrespective of age, it hits hard. It tore out part of my heart that was never replaced. I did not cry much. I was just numb as I felt so bad she died alone. I knew I should have been with her. Somehow, I always thought we would have a few hours' notice, just as there had been when my father died, and Mrs Howard.

John drove me and our children to the morgue, where Mam was lying on a stone slab. We kissed her, did our crying, and I whispered, 'I am late. After all our years together you slipped away without me, with no one to wet your lips or hold your hand.' I continued, 'You gave your life to keep us together and never once thought of yourself, but we will never forget you.' That was the saddest moment of my life.

I wondered how she died, whether she had suffered, and told myself that I would never know. She had long wanted to die and now she was at peace. She had asked for a plain coffin and a simple cross and habit. She categorically asked that we did not get an expensive coffin. I carried out her wishes and arranged the funeral.

The next time I saw her after leaving the hospital, she was in her coffin. Thousands of memories flashed through my mind as I gazed at her. Her face looked at ease. I looked at her folded hands, with the rosary beads wound tightly around her long white fingers, and I thought back on how many times those hands counted the Hail Marys and Holy Marys as she said the rosary.

Then I thought of that iron woman who had picked up a barth of hay and swung it over her shoulder to take to the cows. She had the strength of a horse, yet she did not look strong – she was a thin, wispy woman. I kept looking at her folded hands, imagining all the washing they had done, all the weeds they picked while I sat on her back. I thought too of all the times she had milked cows alone and never once ordered us out to help her. I thought of how she had managed when she lost her child. Of how she had coped with an alcoholic husband. She waited on him right to the end and asked for help from no one. I thought of how, on a Sunday morning, when dressed for Mass, she looked tall, elegant and feminine in that one and only coat she owned. She was a woman never beaten by the everyday troubles.

Mam was buried in Clonlea graveyard with my sister and father. Many years have passed since her death, and even now guilt is never far away. I looked after her from 1969 to 1992, but she had no quality of life after my father died. I wonder how it would have been if she had stayed on her farm. When she moved to Caherconlish to live with us, she had little to do and she hated the washing machine, the hoover and the iron. To her, they wasted electricity. Not having the dignity of work might have affected her, and maybe she would have fared better had she kept her independence and stayed with her own old ways. I feel there is a lesson to be learned there.

One year later, we had more sad news. John's father, Dan O'Mahony, died on 17 September 1993 in Cork University Hospital, after a short illness. He was eighty-four years old and living with his son Timothy and daughter-in-law Mary when he became ill. He was buried in Millstreet graveyard with his wife, Nora. Mr O'Mahony loved working on his farm and learned to drive the tractor when he was seventy. He travelled and worked around Ireland with our men and was a great help to us. We only expected him to work at ground level, but one day I went to Bundoran, and there he was, fitting slates on a sixty-foot-high roof. He worked for months painting at Kylemore Abbey in Connemara, Co. Galway. He was a genuine, hard-working man. He listened to customers and did what they asked. Mr O'Mahony was the last of the grandparents to pass away and was sadly missed by all, especially his grandchildren.

Many clouds were building up around us in Ardnacrusha: I knew that Collins Steeplejacks needed my full attention but was not getting it, and I felt like I was getting burnt out. I wanted to experience life as a full-time, stay-at-home mum, away from the stress, and I felt I could still make it happen. Essco Collins always ran brilliantly from the first day it opened in 1976 over forty years before, and most of the original people were still in place, including the plant manager, accountant and foreman, who had spent their entire working lives there.

I decided that we would retire from Collins Steeplejacks so I went to see a financial adviser who had been recommended to me to discuss our situation. I told him that I was unable to carry on, and his reply was what I wanted to hear: that many had seen it coming and were waiting for something to go wrong. Friends had wondered how I could manage Collins Steeplejacks, Essco Collins, travel, build a golf course, run a bar and restaurant and have so many accidents and operations. They told me to take a look at myself – that one company would be enough.

We decided to tell our staff, who were probably anticipating the news for some time since I had been out of work a lot, that we were retiring and were handing over the reins to one of our foremen. We paid all creditors and then arranged to pass on the work legally through our solicitor. We advised customers, who would have known our men down through the years, and let them choose what they wanted to do. That went well, and it felt like I had left down a very heavy weight.

We were in close contact with the foreman for the first few months to get him on his feet. Then something terrible happened: he had a stroke that left him unable to run the business. I know life is all about twists and turns, but this was surreal. It was very upsetting for him and his family, and it was a setback for us and all involved. Many of the employees began to worry about their positions, and some of them approached Susan and John, asking them to continue Collins Steeplejacks. After some meetings, Susan and John gave their notice to their respective employers, left their full-time jobs and went straight into the steeplejack business. It broke my heart to see Susan give up her teaching post and John his position at the Ardhú Ryan Hotel, but they were free to make their own decisions and part of me was very proud to see Collins Steeplejacks back again.

At first, it was strange to see the company being run without us, but John and I kept out of it and gave Susan and John plenty of scope to see what had to be done and to make whatever changes they wanted. They continued with the same type of work, working on roofs, churches, convents, factories and hospitals, and installing lightning conductors and radomes. Over time they added some additional services, such as renovating heritage buildings and maintaining wind turbines on and off shore.

It was a fascinating time, and an emotional one, but I soon adjusted and left everything in the hands of God. I kept my promise to take things easy but thought numerous times about John and Susan and what they had taken on. I remembered the huge changes and the challenges, and questioned how they would pay for all the training and certification of steeplejacks to keep abreast of the new health and safety regulations.

Their lives were going to be driven by technology and would be very different to ours. Computers, conference calls and mobile phones were becoming the norm. They would have websites, email, Facebook, Twitter and LinkedIn. They could reach vast numbers of customers, engineers and architects. Google could give them up-to-date information on materials and Google Maps and Google Earth showed them any site they were sending their installation crews to.

Then, when we were just about up to date, along came the iPhone to replace satnav, cameras and calculators, and the learning had to begin all over again. Now we wonder what is coming next year and if we will be able to keep abreast. For a steeplejack to be able to photograph a problem on a roof and to forward it to the office and to the customer at the same time means that decisions can be made while they are on the roof fitting slates or attaching a lightning conductor.

Later Mr Cohen received an offer and sold the radome companies to L-3 Communications Inc., Ayer, Massachusetts, who continued manufacturing the product as before and just renamed the companies L-3 Essco USA and L-3 Essco Collins Ltd, Kilkishen. It was wonderful news, and when the new owners visited Ireland we got acquainted and new friendships were made. We thank them for the direct and indirect employment they gave at the factory in Kilkishen and for the radome installation contracts they continue to give to Collins Steeplejacks, especially during the recession.

Visits to and from America decreased after the sale of Mr Cohen's business, but we stayed in regular contact with the family and were delighted that they came to Ireland in 1998 to attend Susan's wedding to Seamus Lynch – and again in 1999 when John married Fiona Dobson. They are like our family and we miss the close contact we had in earlier years, but we are all getting on and that is simply something we have to accept.

In 1996, just when we thought life was going to be easy, another surprise came our way. We had a decision to make about Hilda, who was eleven at the time and studying the violin in Limerick. We were advised by her music teacher to take her to Dublin for further music studies. We were now faced with a decision about moving there to give her that opportunity. Hilda loved classical music and had been successful in competitions at the famous Féilí Luimní held in Limerick each year and the Feis Ceoil in Dublin, among others.

We approached a professor in Dublin for an audition, and he agreed to train her. For the first year, we drove her up and back for that one-hour lesson, but the 120-mile journey each way was difficult, and the professor told her she should be part of his orchestra and part of the music scene in Dublin.

We made the decision to pack our bags again and bought a house in Dundrum, which in 1996 was a small village outside Dublin. In a way, the timing was fine as Martina was at UCD and we could be with her too. We knew that when Hilda finished her Leaving Certificate we could return to Clare if we wished. Twenty years on, the famous Dundrum Town Centre is fifty metres away, and the Luas line, the Beacon Hospital and the M50 motorway are all nearby. It was interesting to observe so much development concentrated in that one area over such a short time. During the Celtic Tiger, many of the factories and large stores in the nearby Stillorgan and Leopardstown industrial estates were demolished and high-rise apartment blocks put in their place. We hardly recognise the area now.

Hilda had two violin lessons a week before school, which meant getting out at 6 a.m., plus theory classes, along with hours spent practising at home and three hours of study for her Leaving Certificate. I knew it would be tough, but she was adamant that this was what she wanted. She studied for her Leaving Certificate at Alexandra College, Milltown, a short distance from Dundrum. She joined their orchestra and practised three to four hours every day. In Transition Year, she practised for six hours each day on top of school work.

John and I drove her to all the competitions around Ireland, and I travelled with her to the Kloster Schöntal International Competition for Violin, in Germany, where she was one of four violinists to represent Ireland. It was an experience for us: Irish competitions usually had only one adjudicator, but this competition had seven adjudicators and two foremen, all from different countries. We were astonished, and not a little disheartened, when a student almost two years younger than the Irish participants won the competition in Hilda's age group. We met with entrants from the UK, the USA, Germany, Israel, Russia, Bulgaria, Romania and China in her age group, but almost every country in the world participated in the competition.

When Hilda completed her Leaving Certificate in 2002, we moved back to Ardnacrusha and she travelled to America to the Cohens and spent time with their daughter Lynn, who had a doctorate in applied behaviour analysis (ABA) and was an expert in the field of psychology. Lynn has served as an ABA consultant for children with autism for twenty years and has designed and overseen intensive ABA programmes for families. She is invited all over the world to lecture on the subject. It was during that summer in Boston that Hilda developed an interest in studying ABA herself and decided, on her return, to do a degree in psychology. After she graduated, she trained for a couple of years in Rathfarnham before going to the UK to do a master's in speech and language therapy combined. She continued to play her violin in the meantime.

One day, I saw Hilda with a computer, and I was curious. We had bought our first computer back in 1985 when John was about fourteen – he was the only person to use it. Now that I had more time, I became interested and did the European Computer Driving Licence course. My teacher was very thorough, and, to my utmost surprise, I was hooked. I bought my own computer and loved making conference calls to John and Susan at home in Clare. I now enjoy fixing problems and have opened up a PC to see the inside and fitted it back together again. I studied more online courses with Kilroy's College, Grand Canal Street, Dublin, and I have one to finish when my book is written. Computing, using the Internet, studying and writing are now what I love most. I am addicted to IT, so my other hobbies of DIY, sewing and knitting are farther down the list.

While Hilda was in school, with time on our hands and computer skills, I volunteered at Our Lady's Hospice in Harold's Cross and was assigned to help patients who wanted to set up email addresses or to look up their medication. On other occasions, my duty was to sit with new patients to settle them in, or to work in the office, typing letters. I also served in the shop. Basically, I did what I was told! John joined me, and he drove patients to the different hospitals for treatment and then collected them when they were finished. He made many friends and was often sad when he would go in the next day to collect them and find that they had passed away during the night. It would restore your faith in humanity to see the wonderful work done by all there, including the volunteers who had been there for many, many years.

I enjoyed more than anything going to Youthreach in Nutgrove, which was not far from Dundrum. Volunteering there was very rewarding because the results were instant. We do not hear enough about these centres, where young people get a second chance at education. Some students learned how to cook, and everyone had a meal there, which encouraged many to attend. I also volunteered a couple of nights a week at the Citizens Information Centre in Dundrum, and that was a mind-boggling experience that taught me how to find all the information anyone could need, legal or otherwise. It was the best way to make friends in a new city and it was enriching giving something back.

I was particularly inspired by one eighty-three-year-old lady I met there. She wanted to buy a computer and learn how to send emails. I set up an email address for her and worked with her until she became familiar with the machine. In no time at all, she was in touch with her son and daughter. It showed me that age was not a barrier to learning computer skills.

At that same time, we became interested in genealogy. One day, John and I set off to visit the various offices and libraries, and we typed up what we found. When we came home to Clare, we went to the graveyards and our local priests, and soon we had enough information to type up the family tree. It took me months to get it finished, and I got confused with my grandfather Collins of Enagh and my dad's mother Collins from Cappanalaght. With so many Collinses it was difficult to unravel. I went to the Clare Heritage and Genealogy Centre in Corofin and met Antoinette, who sorted it out.

Antoinette also told me that we had relations in New Zealand and Australia, which was a real surprise. Ted Collins, the Bishop of Darwin, Australia, had been in touch with her, tracing his ancestors. He had called in person and Antoinette did the family tree for him. Then he had gone in search of his relatives. He was a second cousin to my dad and had several cousins in Ireland. I am sure my parents would have been very surprised to find there was a bishop in the family. We enjoyed meeting him when he returned to Ireland, and he told us that he had been a policeman, like his father before him, and that he had only joined the priesthood when he was twenty-four years old. He was Bishop of Darwin for twenty-one years until his retirement in 2007. He came to Ireland for six weeks, and John took him to Knock Shrine in Co. Mayo and to Donegal to visit the parents of one of the priests in his parish. He also enjoyed a game of golf. We kept in touch with him, and with his sister, Madge, and her daughter, Anne Cleary. It was with deep sadness we learned that he had passed away in August 2014, aged eighty-three.

I have lined up many challenges, and one is to go back to climb Croagh Patrick one more time. I failed twice and went the third time with Martina, who was patient with me and encouraged me to get to the summit. It was the wettest July ever, so coming down was easy, as we fell and slid most of the way.

I will try Lough Derg again, which is tough but enriching. I went there twice and found the fasting hard but enjoyed the praying. I still say the same prayers that my parents taught me and I have passed on to our children and grandchildren. I find solace in my faith, and it is the most important thing in my life. I truly benefit from my belief in God, and a phrase that helps is 'Ask and you shall receive.' However, I would not impose my beliefs on anybody.

A couple of years ago, Maria Mullarkey, who was researching for the popular RTÉ programme *Nationwide*, told us she was in the area and would interview John and Susan. We were delighted to have the publicity and it was the first time that they were interviewed. She was a lovely, down-to-earth lady and made every effort to put us at ease, but we were still nervous.

RTÉ also filmed a series of television programmes on families in business, called *Dynasties*, and we were chosen to be one of the families. Katherine Cahill did the reporting and Hilary Jones was on camera. They knew we found it daunting and tried their best to make it easy, telling us we would get the hang of it, but we didn't, and I don't think I ever will. I thought that as I got older the microphone would not bother me as much, but it still does. We were ready to view it on the night and were pleasantly surprised to hear the voice of the lovely

Mary Kennedy of *Nationwide* narrating, and thankfully it was not obvious to viewers that we were nervous.

I would love to know how people get to be confident speakers. I keep promising myself that I will go to Toastmasters and get some lessons. It is on my to-do list! At my age, I have a great deal of experience and want to pass it on, but I have a fear of microphones and am always critical of my accent. I want to change that as it is nice to listen to confident speakers like those we hear on television.

I loved meeting our very own down-to-earth television personality Marty Whelan and with him Ciana Campbell, who was great to chat to, when I was doing an interview for their show. It helped that Ciana's husband knew about a radome we fitted in Baldonnel. I was calm enough because there were others there who were nervous too. It was for the midday show *12 to 1*, which reached a new audience for me.

I was also asked on a Saturday morning children's programme with Aonghus McAnally. Aonghus was a very young man then. I am sure I didn't contribute much – you need to be funny for small children. I showed them photos of a steeplejack and talked about our work. It went off okay – I felt no threat and there were no awkward questions. Children are more knowledgeable now than we were at their age, and when they come on television some amaze me with their confidence.

I met Seán Duignan when I was working on the installation of a radome in Schull, Co. Cork (which was blown up soon after, on 20 September 1982). RTÉ filmed us fitting panels for *News Round Up*. Seán asked the steeplejacks what they thought of a female boss, and they replied that you do not need to be shown what to do if you know your trade, so it doesn't matter whether the boss is a man or a woman. They were not afraid of the cameras or of speaking, which amazed me. After that television appearance, other articles appeared in women's magazines and I was asked to give talks at many women's functions throughout Ireland.

Some time later, in 1987, Aileen O'Toole wrote a book called *The Pace Setters*, which was another boost and kept the Collins Steeplejacks name out there. Then, to my delight, I was contacted by another writer, Maxine Jones, to include us in her book, *Successful Irish Businesswomen*, which was published in 1992.

Life was good, until, in 2006, we were in Portugal with Mr Cohen's daughter Lynn, her husband, Kevin Brennan, and their son, Ben, when the news came that her father was very ill. They packed up and returned to the USA immediately and arrived just in time to be with him when he passed away on 25 November 2006. We flew home to Ireland and then on to Boston for the funeral. It was a very sad occasion – and the end of an era for us.

Mr Albert Cohen had been a true friend and leader, and he was truly missed. He had a dynamic personality and was an inspiration to all. I relied on him for advice about our company, legal and financial. He loved his product and travelled the world to sell it. He was a very successful entrepreneur and businessman, who had time for everyone, rich and poor, and that was reflected in the large attendance at his funeral. He got a heartfelt send-off from Anna; their three daughters, Lynn, Missy and Bambi; sons-in-laws, Kevin, Doug and David; and grandchildren, Ben, Andrew, Joshua, Max and Anna. His former employees, friends and customers were all there to say the final goodbye and to pay their respects.

In the eulogy, we were reminded that Mr Cohen was a genius at mathematics and a most respected figure in the radome industry and in the field of astronomy. He was always planning a new business or trying to find a better way of doing things and never tired of passing on practical advice. There was never a sound during his speeches because he always had something new to say and, very often, a few surprises. He often gave talks for the IDA and for other Irish government bodies about joint ventures and doing business in Ireland. He was the co-founder of the Essco radome business and the founder in 1996 of the Essco Massachusetts General Hospital Breast Cancer Research Fund. He had the courage to set up a joint venture in a small village in Ireland in 1974 that gave employment and opportunities to many, and we are very grateful to him.

Three years on, John and I were enjoying life, like most people of our age. We had invested our money in property after selling the golf and leisure centre and were earning an income. We were occasionally busy looking after our tenants in the rental properties we had invested in, but we felt under no pressure. We had four grandchildren, all under seven, whom we loved beyond words. They were in a crèche, but we took them most days to spend time with them. I was sixty-six years old and very fit, swimming and cycling regularly. I had been to Weight Watchers and had lost a stone so I was not overweight.

Suddenly, our world fell apart. We were in Portugal in a

friend's apartment, and, as one does, I was being really careful, cleaning and ensuring every place was perfect when I noticed a dark blood discharge. I can say with 100 per cent certainty that I would not have seen it if I had been busily working at home. I had no pain or discomfort.

Prior to this I had booked myself for a routine colonoscopy. There was a long delay, but I was not worried. I called regularly and was still not near the top of the list. However, once I saw signs of blood, we booked the next flight home. Every spare moment I was on my mobile trying to book a colonoscopy – even at the airport while waiting for the flight. I called ump-teen hospitals all over Ireland and was told the waiting list was three to six weeks and even longer in places. I did not give up. I explained to all that it was not a routine check, that I had signs of cancer, and eventually I struck luck when I called the Bon Secours in Tralee. They had a cancellation or were sympathetic and took my story seriously – whatever, I was really glad.

I only had a day to prepare. Susan met us off the flight with the medication I needed for the procedure, and I started drinking it. John drove me to Tralee the next morning, 10 September 2009, and he walked around for six hours while I was inside. When the procedure was over, I watched Dr Jane English visit each bed and discharge patient after patient. Soon the large ward was empty except for me. I was the second patient to be admitted that morning, so being left till last was not a good sign.

I saw Dr English walk away without coming to me, which left me in no doubt but that I had cancer and that I only needed to hear how bad it was. I was there for about fifteen minutes, which felt like the longest time ever endured. Then a nurse asked me to come with her to Dr English's office. She opened the office door, sympathetically pointed to the chair and left.

Dr English came in and asked who was with me. I told her that I had telephoned my husband and that he was outside but that I did not want him there as we didn't discuss these types of things. I told her that for our forty-three years of marriage John and I had never discussed health issues or pregnancies, so this was the way I wanted it. I said I would be really embarrassed if he was there and asked her to give me the result, that I was able for it, but she just got up from behind her desk and went to fetch him. It was really difficult then – I thought John would faint talking about body parts, especially given where the problem was.

Well, we sat side by side, facing her, and with the most compassionate face she leaned out over her desk, as if meeting us half way, and said, 'You were not expecting a normal result.' I told her no, and she told me that I had colon cancer. While I was expecting bad news, pure shock would not describe how I felt right then. Hearing the words put me in total despair, which was unlike me. It was the word 'cancer'. It had that awful, indescribable effect. Death, not hope, came to mind. Life stood still.

Her office and desk, her words, her face, are still ingrained in my mind to this very day. With her pen and an A4 sheet (which I still have), she drew where the cancer was and explained what had to be done. Straight away, she began making arrangements to get it removed. I told her I was going back to Limerick, and she gave me the sketch, telling me to give it to whatever surgeon I was going to. A report would be typed and sent out, but it might take another ten days, so best to use the sketch. She told me she would send on the result of the biopsy. She was so efficient; she knew how important time is with cancer – it's growing and growing, and survival can be all about time.

Dr English was in no hurry with me – she was just amazing. She invited questions, and I had lots, but I did not have the strength to ask them. I just told her how grateful I was to her that she had a cancellation because waiting would have been terrible. I decided to scream later in a quiet place, but right then I held it together. As we drove out the road, not a word was spoken. I knew that I had to tell my family. They were all adults and I was grateful for that.

There is no right or wrong way to tell your family you have cancer. Eventually I called Susan and John at home in Clare. They knew I had gone for the check-up and that I was suspicious, but they were dumbfounded when I delivered the news and there were tears. I got some relief sharing the problem with them. Then I called Martina and Hilda in Dublin. They were in a different position to Susan and John, who were their own bosses. Though Martina and Hilda were in work, they dealt with the news the best they could.

Once home in Ardnacrusha, I decided to get as much information as I could and visited the Irish Cancer Society at Limerick University Hospital. I talked with friends and family who had survived cancer, with some who were living with it, with others who were going through chemo treatment, and with a dear friend who had just had his own surgery and who, though dealing with his own fear, was really reassuring.

My friends were outstanding. They gave me their stories and advised me on what to do. Words could not explain the comfort those people gave me. It was wonderful to have them to talk to as they were the ones who truly understood the shock and the fear.

One friend of over forty years in particular was unusual, given that she was dying. I didn't want to burden her, but she would have found out from someone else and that would have been worse. We always phoned each other and had worked on many projects together, and I visited her regularly. She started the conversation with, 'Have you a pen and paper, Angela?' and gave me a list of things to do and questions to ask the doctor. She passed away shortly afterwards and I miss her dearly. I remember her so often now, and I cannot recall ever meeting anyone so brave and with so much to give.

My dear friends the Cohens were on the phone often, offering all kinds of good advice. They told me I could pay for a conference call with a cancer expert in Massachusetts General Hospital and get another opinion, and that for a small fee I could send my file there and call back later to talk to an expert – a valuable and comforting service and one I was not aware of until they told me about it.

After I had talked to everyone, I weighed up all the options about where to go for the removal of my cancer. I was advised first to go to a consultant in Dublin, and did so, but he would not accept the colonoscopy from Tralee and wanted to book me in to do his own, which meant delaying the operation, duplication and more waiting and expense, none of which impressed me.

When I was finished my discussion with him, he and John began a conversation about the upcoming All-Ireland Final on 20 September, predicting who was going to win and getting very excited about the result. They went on and on until I interrupted and asked if we could leave. I felt very hurt and was in a bad place with very little patience. Needless to say, I didn't get him to treat me.

I went back to Dr Richard O'Flaherty. He was my parents' doctor and a friend and neighbour. Dr O'Flaherty recommended Dr Eoin Condon in Limerick University Hospital, and Orla, his secretary, made an appointment for me. What a difference from the last experience. Dr Condon was a kind, caring, down-to-earth doctor with a lovely personality. He was an expert in keyhole surgery, and he took the colonoscopy result from Tralee and spoke with Dr English. He was very detailed in his explanation of what he was going to do, how he was going to remove the cancer and what the consequences would be. He too sketched where the cancer was. Then he got on with the removal so there was no delay or extra expense.

There was just one small problem. While Dr Condon was a Limerick man, he was working in Ohio at the time and was only home in Ireland for a short while. He explained that he would have to return to the USA immediately after the operation. I told him that this was fine; I was not worried about the aftercare – I was just happy to get the cancer removed. I was so obsessed with it, I thought I could feel it growing. The operation was successful. I got no infection and received excellent care. When I was in hospital, I asked to have no visitors apart from John and my children. I worried that one of the grandchildren might get infected with MRSA or a contagious disease.

Twelve days later, I was home recovering, feeling wonderful, when I received a call from a doctor in the hospital to say I had cysts in my liver and that he was sending me for an ultrasound. I asked when would I have that and he told me it would be ten days or more – he would let me know.

I was devastated as I knew about metastases, where cancer can enter your bloodstream and go to the liver and lymph nodes. Again, I called my friends, and John's sister Mary told me I could get an ultrasound in the Crescent in Limerick. I was able to go there immediately. There and then I was told that my cysts were benign and that I had nothing to worry about. They could have been there for years and were harmless. I was overjoyed – there are no words to explain that news. I had no biopsy as the ultrasound said that the cysts were benign.

After the surgery, I was referred to Professor Rajnish Gupta, Director of Cancer Services at the Mid-western Regional Hospital in Limerick. He told me that research had shown that women with T2 cancer who had chemo were the same after five years as those who did not have it. I got a second opinion and was advised to take my chances, to go with the research and not to have any chemo as it might destroy good cells and do more harm than good.

In earlier years, before my diagnosis, I organised a couple of colonoscopies for John, but after going to see the doctor and paying the fee he always cancelled the day before. I was really concerned for him, but little did I know that I was the one who should have had the check-up. It does not necessarily follow that those with cancer in their family should go for checks. Everyone over fifty should. Early detection is the cure. I still have to convince John to take the test, and it is on my 'to do' list.

Six months after my cancer was removed I was recalled for a colonoscopy and got the all-clear. Then I had to go once a year for four and a half years, which I did. I was really happy that they were all clear and thank God for this.

In 2010, after having a colonoscopy, it was recommended that I go for an angiogram since heart disease is in my family. I went to the heart specialist, Dr Charles McCreery, for the procedure, and he discovered that I had three blocked valves. I returned later to have an angioplasty and three stents fitted. Back then, this was done through the groin. It was quite a simple procedure and painless. I was awake and talking to the doctor and nurse right through. I felt only pressure for a few moments.

Afterwards, I was warned to lay still, and they kept a weight on the area of the groin where the insertion had been made. That was the only inconvenience. It was stress-free, and I had an overnight hospital stay. I just had to take all of my tablets for my high blood pressure and a blood thinning tablet for a year. Dr McCreery was a wonderful, skilled specialist with an outstanding bedside manner. This experience also proved that regular check-ups are really necessary even though we may feel no pain. I would not have known about these blockages only that I had had cancer, and one check led to another and possibly prevented a heart attack. Somehow, hearing about blockages and heart attacks did not strike the same fear in me as cancer.

Five years later, on 25 January 2015, I had a heart attack and suffered a lot until the diagnosis was made. I had another stent fitted on the same valve, but once the stent was fitted and the blood could flow, the pain stopped and the procedure was painless. Again, it took about an hour. On this occasion it was done through a vein in my wrist, which was much easier as I could move my body and shift around and had only to keep my wrist still. I had it done nearer to home – at the Galway Clinic, by Mr Gordon Pate, who was very skilled and really compassionate.

9

Looking Back
and Lessons Learned

In the 1960s, as a young girl of twenty-three and a managing director, I did not expect to be taken seriously so I often dressed as a man when on site and slipped around unnoticed. On the odd occasion in 1968, when I was noticeably pregnant, there were a few awkward moments at a first meeting, but once we started to talk business it became normal.

I felt it was a benefit being a female as I was offered the courtesy of speaking first and I was always allowed in to factories, presbyteries and convents even though I did not always have an appointment. There was a great respect for women in those days, to the point that some men raised their hats when women passed, and, if dining out, some men stood up at the table until the women sat down or when they left. That happens in some places to this day, but of course women do not expect it.

Being a female steeplejack was the reason we got so much publicity. The point was proven when I was awarded large contracts. Yet, when we were on site, we all worked as a team, and the steeplejacks did not feel they had to mind me. So it was certainly no handicap being a woman in a man's world. I deeply appreciated customers, some of whom were very large companies, giving me work and trusting me at a time when it was unheard of to have a young, pregnant woman doing site work.

I am very thankful to those who work in Collins Steeplejacks and those who worked with us in Essco Collins, the golf and leisure centre and the Angler's Rest. I remember with fondness the way we worked and socialised together, sharing highs and lows. It was never employer and employee, just us. I prayed that no one would be injured and, thankfully, no one ever was, and I hope that will continue.

Some of the employees of those companies travelled with John and me, and some went on their own to work all around Ireland and the world. It was often lonely to be away from home for long periods, but everyone did it willingly. Partners took full responsibility for the children and the home in their absence. I was very close to those mothers and appreciate what they did to help our company. I remember especially the deceased steeplejacks, and we reminisce about them and think of what we all have learned from life.

I learned from my parents and saw the sacrifices they made, and I tried to imitate them. Coming from a small farming background had advantages: it made me thrifty and, having little, I was grateful for everything I did have. I learned from my father that alcohol destroys homes and we did not follow in his footsteps. He was a neat worker and I tried to learn from that. He always said, 'It is just as easy to do something right as wrong.' We acquired a love for music and dancing from him.

From my mother I learned how to sew, how to work hard and how to have patience and perseverance. I learned that there was nothing a woman could not do. Both my parents taught me the importance of prayer.

Neighbours made time for us and welcomed us into their homes where we learned kindness and manners. One in particular taught me to save a little of my wages each week. I apply that advice when giving talks: I always tell students and graduates to open a bank account and to put in some small amount every week to show consistency. It will assist in getting a loan in later years, and it gives a history of the person and shows responsibility and commitment. Neighbours also told us not to use bad language because, though it might get us attention and make people laugh, it would not guarantee success or promotion.

My teachers taught us the Ten Commandments, which I found to be the basis for a happy life. Honour your parents, respect yourselves, your school, your community and country, they always said. Being true to oneself gives inner peace. My teacher in Limerick told us to be on time for work and never to miss days by pretending to be sick if we were not. It would encourage others to do likewise, and that, in turn, would affect productivity. We were to value work as it brought dignity. We were taught to always say 'no problem' and to show a willingness to carry out a task and to look up to employers and ensure that they never had to carry out tasks that secretaries could do. Their time was better spent planning the company's future. This applies now more than ever as there is so much competition with Ireland from other countries.

The training I received in my first job set me up for life. It may have been tough on occasion, but it was a great start. Mr Lynch often said there was no point telling him I could not do something – if I could not do my work and run his office, then I was not to bother collecting my wages. He was correct. If managers are responsible and efficient, then employees usually follow. The old people would say, if it is wrong at the top it will be wrong at the bottom.

I looked on Mr Cohen as a customer and part-employer, even though we were partners. I learned about international business from him. He insisted we had to go out there and sell. I had to find the courage to push myself as I was out of my depth. I noticed that some customers required more time than others. Some needed to be visited often in order to get acquainted, while others wanted us to come straight to the point. Mr Cohen taught me that most business was done through friendship and trust. When the Chinese delegation visited the Essco Collins factory at Kilkishen in 1979, we received only one large order, but that visit and business brought publicity to the Munster region, especially Clare, Limerick and North Tipperary. It ensured that those areas are well known in China – so much so that in February 2012, when Mr Xi Jinping, the Chinese Vice-President, visited Ireland, he actually landed in Shannon and asked to visit Sixmilebridge, which is four miles from the L-3 Essco Collins factory where the first ever Chinese delegation visited in 1979. Thirty-seven years later, they are still coming back.

John and Susan have been running Collins Steeplejacks for over twenty years. They are heritage contractors and carry out regular maintenance work on hospitals, churches, convents and factories. Although the manufacture of radomes has discontinued, Collins Steeplejacks still get contracts for the installation of radomes as far away as Japan and as near as the UK. Susan and her husband, Seamus, have one son, Andy. John and his wife, Fiona, have three daughters: Kate, Emma and Karen. I am delighted they stayed in the area and we can see them all the time.

Hilda is a classically trained violinist. She teaches violin and plays at concerts, weddings, conferences and corporate functions. Martina is a solicitor in Dublin and loves her life there. She runs marathons. We enjoy going to support her and wonder how a slip of a girl can run twenty-six miles in a little over three hours.

I feel John and I have spent a couple of lifetimes together since we met in 1965, over fifty years ago. We worked together in the office, on site, travelling and in our home, often talking about the business from morning till night. I could never have succeeded without him. He left me completely in charge of our finances as he had no interest and let me make important decisions. He was nearly always up for a challenge. He learned to cook and has fed me for the past five years while I was working on my book. He did the spell-check many times and proofread it and gave me his opinion.

I set out in life with no five-year plan and no degree. John and I did not have any regard for money or for being successful – we just enjoyed the challenges and achievements and meeting wonderful, compassionate people along the way. People have asked me over the years about the qualities that made me an entrepreneur. I never know how to reply, except to say 'pure determination'. You need to be a risk taker, to have a skill with solving problems and, above all, to be flexible and to never give up. I worked long hours and used common sense, taking every opportunity that came my way.

You need to be dedicated and able to take reasonable risks, to be optimistic and to surround yourself with like-minded people. Then you need to think business day and night. I was a workaholic and pushed myself to the limit, but that is not always necessary.

You can come from nowhere and go anywhere. You do not have to come from a rich or famous background to start a successful business or to get access to financial support.

I loved being an employee and an employer. Being able to take orders is a fine quality and can take you to the apex of your career. There are many who cannot take orders, so becoming an entrepreneur is an excellent option that has many benefits. Teamwork is important, and employers need to acknowledge staff for their contribution and include them in decisions. (Sometimes this is as important as a salary increase.)

Just as this book was going to print, we received news that the factory in Kilkishen was closing. While this is sad, it is worth remembering that we had over forty years of employment for the very loyal staff of L-3 Essco Collins Ltd, most of whom spent their entire working lives there. The company is keeping its marketing and installation departments in Ireland, which will ensure the bond is not broken.

We had been anticipating that day for quite a while, especially when we saw so many large companies leaving to manufacture in low-cost countries. When we began in 1975, we had little competition, but now many companies are manufacturing radomes. I know L-3 took this action to stay competitive and to do their best for their shareholders.

However, good news came when I received a call from them to say that they will donate the building to my charity. The very vibrant community and I express gratitude for this generous offer, and we are exploring opportunities for another investor for the plant. In this latter stage of my life, I am extremely complimented to be involved in this new endeavour.

Acknowledgements

My thanks to the Irish media, the radio and television pre-
senters and interviewers, journalists, researchers, newspapers
and magazines too numerous to mention, who, from the early
1960s, were interested in the unusual life of a female steeplejack working in a man's world. The publicity I received from
them led to Essco Inc. (now L-3 Communications Essco) hiring Collins Steeplejacks to work around the world for them,
and also to the building of the Essco Collins radome manufacturing plant in Kilkishen in 1975, providing much-needed
employment to the area.

My thanks also to Veuve Clicquot, who awarded me Business Woman of the Year in 1980 (and to Gilbeys Distillers,
who sponsored the event), to the Bowmaker Bank for the
Bowmaker Award for Irish Industry in 1986, and to the Board
of the NCEA/HETAC, who conferred me with an Honorary
Doctorate in 1992. These honours opened many doors for me.

I am grateful to the following people for their support
throughout my career: Noel Cassidy and Duncan Gray, who
guided us through building our 9-hole golf course, with
encouragement from the locals all around Clonlara and the
people of Limerick; Christy O'Connor Jnr (RIP), who offi-
cially opened our golf course; all of my wonderful and dedicated staff, both living and deceased; Mr Albert Cohen, his
wife, Anna, and family; Carlo Mistretta, the first man I met

from Essco, in 1969; all my customers, both in Ireland and abroad, especially those who believed in me when I was in my twenties and doing a man's work; Maxine Jones; Aileen O'Toole; and Mr Lynch (RIP), my first employer, who took me on at sixteen and trained me.

I would also like to acknowledge the support of the following organisations: IDA, Enterprise Ireland, FÁS (now Solas), IIRS, Elevate PR, Thoms Directory, the Department of Foreign Affairs, the Department of Transport, Bord Fáilte, Clare Development Association, Kilkishen Cultural Centre, various chambers of commerce, the Council for the Status of Women, the Women's Talent Bank, Probus, Zonta and the ICA.

I would like to thank the following people and organisations, who kindly provided images for the book: the *Limerick Leader*, Dermot Lynch and his colleagues, *Limerick Post*, *Limerick Chronicle*, *Clare Champion*, *Clare Echo*, *Clare People*, *Irish Independent*, *Sunday Independent*, *The Irish Times*, *The Sunday Times*, *The Cork Examiner*, *Evening Echo*, Egliston Photographic Agency, Press 22, Cormac Byrne, Michael Martin, Eamonn O'Connor (RIP), the Limerick photo centre, Franks, Dan Lenihan, Brooks of Ennis, Mac Gill Photographers, Coe Photographers, Dermot Hurley, and P & M Photographers, Ardagh.

Finally my thanks to all those who encouraged me to write this book and who stayed patient with me, offering advice and guidance: my neighbours, the many proofreaders who were so helpful, one in particular who read it during her long stay in hospital, my editor, Liz Hudson, and my publishers, Mercier Press.

With so many people to thank it is possible I have forgotten someone, but it was not intentional and I apologise if I have.

I fondly recall you all and include you in my prayers.